THE DILEMMA
OF WILDERNESS

THE DILEMMA OF WILDERNESS

by
Corry McDonald

Sunstone Press
Santa Fe, New Mexico

This book is dedicated to those friends who have had
the patience to listen to and heed my concerns for their
public lands and to those folks who have told me of
their vexations at what they consider unjust regulations
of public lands, particularly Wilderness.

Drawings by David Linson Berry

Library of Congress Cataloging in Publication Data:

McDonald, Corry, 1914-
    The dilemma of wilderness.

    Bibliography: p. 111
    Includes index.
    1. Wilderness areas--United States. 2. Wilderness
areas--Law and legislation--United States. I. Title.
QH76.M384   1986   333.7'82'0973   86-5839
ISBN 0-86534-088-9

Published in 1987 by SUNSTONE PRESS
            Post Office Box 2321
            Santa Fe, NM 87504-2321 / USA

CONTENTS

INTRODUCTION

M an first came 30,000 years ago to North America across the Bering land bridge where Alaska and Siberia now almost meet. So we are told.[1]

Spear or harpoon heads have been reported as findings in the skeletal remains of animals in Alaska. Attempts at dating such finds have been made. The weapon heads do appear to be man-made, thus implying that man was indeed present and hungry at an early date. The dominant fossils were those of mammoths and they appear to have been living in the Pleistocine period. There was one case in particular in Moravia of cave paintings depicting Paleolithic man hunting and killing elephants.

Those hunters looked out upon a vast de facto wilderness. It was a dilemma to him then and even more so for modern man; tales of the wilderness dilemma have been carried down from generation to generation. The Icelandic Sagas of the 9th and 10th centuries were one of the early heroic recordings.[2] The Egyptian cuneiform writings and the secrets of the Rosetta Stone permitted transposition of many an early tale of man's endeavors of taming the wilderness in early times.

Wilderness, or man's initial unmodified environment, had its own rules in many ways in that environment presented him with at least two or more equally unsatisfactory alternatives. He could either work or starve, hunt or gather, fight or flee. He could bake in the sun or hide from it in a cave. He seemed to find himself in a predicament that made him uncomfortable most of the time. Civilization has overcome many of those unsatisfactory alternatives but has introduced new ones in today's wilderness. That is what this book attempts to survey.

Today's American wilderness is also a paradox in which it is seemingly contradictory and yet is perhaps true. It is also an enigma to many of the wilderness users and lovers. Wilderness is a paradox, dilemma, and an enigma; hard to understand, as it is for those wanting to tame the wilderness, is the thrust of this book. In some cases, legislation has been resorted to for the purpose of alleviating the dilemma but that has only deepened it for some potential users. Lawsuits have been initiated to solve some users' dilemmas. Regulations have been promulgated by some of the Public Land Agencies to control abuses arising from parts of the dilemmas.

Currently throughout the world, man has reduced the wilderness to perhaps less than 25% of the land area. There are vast expanses of the earth's surfaces without a mark of man. These frontiers are being beaten back by an ever more technologically capable human species. We are even populating the Antarctic continent.

The United States, in less than five hundred years, has changed from about 98% wilderness to something like 5% wilderness. When the heavily armed Cortez stepped ashore in eastern Mexico in the early 1500s, there were some areas populated sparsely by Indian tribes. Indian dwellings, villages, cities, routes, roads, cultivated fields, and annually burned areas made up the marks of man in the continent-wide wilderness.

In our own day the continental United States, or more exactly the lower forty-eight, contains about two percent enacted National Wilderness with perhaps another three or four percent de facto wilderness remaining.[3] We may change the rules and enact a larger percentage than three or four on the basis that a natural recovery of marginal areas can be made in time, that the marks of man will fade with the natural rejuvenation processes. Hopefully, man will learn to restrain himself to allow that last vestige of wilderness to go undefiled. That is part of the dilemma.

During the late 1800s and early 1900s a small but growing segment of the population became concerned about the rapidly dwindling natural countryside which to them was America, the unspoiled. A wilderness ethic grew and they became vocal enough to describe their dilemma to the Congress. It took many years, several decades in fact, until Congress passed the Wilderness Act (see Chapter 1). This legislation was intended to alleviate the dwindling wilderness dilemma, but it introduced some new dimensions to the problem.

National Wilderness is that which has been enacted by the Congress of the United States in accordance with the Wilderness Act of 1964, Public Law 88-577. In 1985 there were twenty-one National

Wilderness Areas in New Mexico. The total area comes to 1,535,268 acres, or 1.98% of the area of the state. There are several de facto areas not yet enacted.[4]

Users of these areas, as well as potential users, are faced with unsatisfactory alternatives depending upon their interests and viewpoints. Wilderness lovers can destroy the very pristine quality they seek, through overuse or unwitting abuse. Miners, seeking mineral riches, can no longer freely cast about in National Wilderness in their search for the mother lode. Oil and gas prospectors are prevented from drilling exploratory wells in Wilderness with a captial W. The Armed Forces are hampered in their training maneuvers by Wilderness restrictions. Cattle growers are limited in the number of cattle they can graze in Wilderness. State Departments of Game and Fish are restricted in many ways from doing their jobs in Wilderness. Horseback transits and associated pack trains are regulated to varying degrees by the Area Managers. Public Land Agencies recognize the Wilderness Dilemma as they manage and administer the Wilderness Areas.

Timber cutting on a commercial basis is not allowed in Wilderness. Firewood cutting and gathering is not allowed. Removal of crashed airplanes is carefully specified in each case by Wilderness Managers, as are crashed hang gliders and balloons carrying passengers or scientific equipment.

Off-road-vehicles, including mountain bicycles, are excluded by law or regulation from Wilderness. All kinds of devices such as "buck trucks" (platforms on a bicycle wheel) used by hunters to haul game, are prohibited. Motor boats are not to be used in Wilderness waters. Motor powered trail makers are not permitted. Chain saws are not used in Wildernesses. Only life and death emergencies can be the basis for the Wilderness Manager at the Regional Forester's level to permit such equipment to be used. Motorized hoists have been used by Search and Rescue parties under such circumstances. These and other threats to the Wilderness condition may make one wonder how any Wilderness can survive. The subsequent chapters attempt to shed light upon these and other dilemmas of Wilderness uses.

CHAPTER 1
Wilderness, A Legal Entity

Congress listened to the pros and cons of National Wilderness for several years before they finally enacted the Wilderness Act of 1964. (See *Wilderness — A New Mexico Legacy*, Sunstone Press, Santa Fe, N.M., 1985.) Thus Congress attempted to alleviate the dilemma before it started. However, like many laws, it is not known and recognized by everyone. The complete text of the Wilderness Act follows.

COMPLETE TEXT OF THE WILDERNESS ACT

Public Law 88-577
88th Congress, S. 4
September 3, 1964

An Act

To establish a National Wilderness Preservation System for the permanent good of the whole people, and for other purposes.

Be it enacted by the Senate and House of Representatives of the United States of America in Congress assembled,

SHORT TITLE

Section. 1. This Act may be cited as the "Wilderness Act."

WILDERNESS SYSTEM ESTABLISHED — STATEMENT OF POLICY

Section 2. (a) In order to assure that an increasing population, accompanied by expanding settlement and growing mechanization, does not occupy and modify all areas within the United States and its possesions, leaving no lands designated for preservation and protection in their natural condition, it is hereby declared to be the policy of the Congress to secure for the American people of present and future generations the benefits of an enduring resource of wilderness. For this purpose there is hereby established a National Wilderness Preservation System to be composed of federally owned areas designated by Congress as "wilderness areas," and these shall be administered for the use and enjoyment of the American people in such manner as will leave them unimpaired for future use and enjoyment as wilderness, and so as to provide for the protection of these areas, the preservation of their wilderness character, and for the gathering and dissemination of information regarding their use and enjoyment as wilderness; and no Federal lands shall be designated as "wilderness areas" except as provided for in this Act or by a subsequent Act.

(b) The inclusion of an area in the National Wilderness Preservation System notwithstanding, the area shall continue to be managed by the Department and agency having jurisdiction thereover immediately before its inclusion in the National Wilderness Preservation System unless otherwise provided by Act of Congress. No appropriation shall be available for the payment of expenses or salaries for the administration of the National Wilderness Preservation System as a separate unit nor shall any appropriations be available for additional personnel stated as being required solely for the purpose of managing or administering areas solely because they are included within the National Wilderness Preservation System.

DEFINITION OF WILDERNESS

(c) A wilderness, in contrast with those areas where man and his own works dominate the landscape, is hereby recognized as an area where the earth and its community of life are untrammeled by man, where man himself is a visitor who does not remain. An area of wilderness is further defined to mean in this Act an area of undeveloped Federal land retaining its primeval character and influence, without permanent improvements or human habitation, which is protected and managed so as to preserve its natural conditions and which (1) generally appears to have been affected primarily by the forces of nature, with the imprint of man's work substantially unnoticeable; (2) has outstanding opportunities for solitude or a primitive and unconfined type of recreation; (3) has at least five thousand acres of land or is of sufficient size as to make practicable its preservation and use in an unimpaired condition; and (4) may also contain ecological, geological, or other features of scientific, educational, scenic, or historical value.

NATIONAL WILDERNESS PRESERVATION SYSTEM — EXTENT OF SYSTEM

SECTION 3. (a) All areas within the national forests classified at least 30 days before the effective date of this Act by the Secretary of Agriculture or the Chief of the Forest Service as "wilderness," "wild," or "canoe" are hereby designated as wilderness areas. The Secretary of Agriculture

12

shall—

(1) Within one year after the effective date of this Act, file a map and legal description of each wilderness area with the Interior and Insular Affairs Committees of the United States Senate and the House of Representatives, and such descriptions shall have the same force and effect as if included in this Act: Provided, however, That correction of clerical and typographical errors in such legal descriptions and maps may be made.

(2) Maintain, available to the public, records pertaining to said wilderness areas, including maps and legal descriptions, copies of regulations governing them, copies of public notices of, and reports submitted to Congress regarding pending additions, eliminations, or modifications. Maps, legal descriptions, and regulations pertaining to wilderness areas within their respective jurisdictions also shall be available to the public in the offices of regional foresters, national forest supervisors, and forest rangers.

Classification. (b) The Secretary of Agriculture shall, within ten years after the enactment of this Act, review, as to its suitability or non-suitability for preservation as wilderness, each area in the national forests classified on the effective date of this Act by the Secretary of Agriculture or the Chief of the Forest Service as "primitive" and report his findings to the President.

Presidential recommendation to Congress. The President shall advise the United States Senate and House of Representatives of his recommendations with respect to the designation as "wilderness" or other reclassification of each area on which review has been completed, together with maps and a definition of boundaries. Such advice shall be given with respect to not less than one-third of all the areas now classified as "primitive" within three years after the enactment of this Act, not less than two-thirds within seven years after the enactment of this Act, and the remaining areas within ten years after the enactment of this Act.

Congressional approval. Each recommendation of the President for designation as "wilderness" shall become effective only if so provided by an Act of Congress. Areas classified as "primitive" on the effective date of this Act shall continue to be administered under the rules and regulations affecting such areas on the effective date of this Act until Congress has determined otherwise. Any such area may be increased in size by the President at the time he submits his recommendations to the Congress by not more than five thousand acres with no more than one thousand two hundred and eighty acres of such increase in any one compact unit; if it is proposed to increase the size of any such area by more than five thousand acres or by more than one thousand two hundred and eighty acres in any one compact unit the increase in size shall not become effective until acted upon by Congress. Nothing herein contained shall limit the President in proposing, as part of his recommendations to Congress, the alteration of exisiting boundaries of primitive areas or recommending the addition of any contiguous area of national forest lands predominantly of wilderness value. Notwithstanding any other provisions of this Act, the Secretary of Agriculture may complete his review and delete such area as may be necessary, but not to exceed seven thousand acres, from the southern tip of the Gore Range-Eagles Nest Primitive Area, Colorado, if the Secretary determines that such action is in the public interest.

Report to President. (c) Within ten years after the effective date of this Act the Secretary of the Interior shall review every roadless area of five thousand contiguous acres or more in the national parks, monuments and other units of the national park system and every such area of, and every roadless island within, the national wildlife refuges and game ranges, under his jurisdiction on the effective date of this Act and shall report to the President his recommendation as to the suitability or non-suitability of each such area or island for preservation as wilderness.

Presidential recommendation to Congress. The President shall advise the President of the Senate and the Speaker of the House of Representatives of his recommendation with respect to the designation as wilderness of each such area or island on which review has been completed, together with a map thereof and a definition of its boundaries. Such advice shall be given with respect to not less than one-third of the areas and islands to be reviewed under this subsection within three years after enactment of this Act, not less than two-thirds within seven years of enactment of this Act, and the remainder within ten years of enactment of this Act.

Congressional approval. A recommendation of the President for designation as wilderness shall become effective only if so provided by an Act of Congress. Nothing contained herein shall, by implication or otherwise, be construed to lessen the present statutory au ority of the Secretary of the Interior with respect to the maintenance o oadless areas within units of the national park system.

Suitability. (d) (1) The Secretary of Agriculture and the Se retary of the Interior shall, prior to submitting any recommendations to ie President with respect to the suitability of any area for preservation as wilderness—

Publication in Federal Register. (A) give such public notice of the proposed action as they deem appropriate, including publication in the Federal Register and in a newspaper having general circulation in the area or areas in the vicinity of the affected land;

Hearings. (B) hold a public hearing or hearings at a location or locations convenient to the area affected. The hearings shall be announced through such means as the respective Secretaries involved deem appropriate, including notices in the Federal Register and in newspapers of general circulation in the area: Provided. That if the lands involved are located in more than one State, at least one hearing shall be held in each State in which a portion of the land lies;

(C) at least thirty days before the date of a hearing advise the Governor of each State and the governing board of each county, or in Alaska the borough, in which the lands are located, and Federal departments and agencies concerned, and invite such officials and Federal agencies to submit their views on the proposed action at the hearing or by no later than thirty days following the date of the hearing.

(2) Any views submitted to the appropriate Secretary under the provisions of (1) of this subsection with respect to any area shall be included with any recommendations to the President and to Congress with respect to such area.

Proposed modification. (e) Any modification or adjustment of boundaries of any wilderness area shall be recommended by the appropriate Secretary after public notice of such proposal and public hearing or hearings as provided in subsection (d) of this section. The proposed modification or adjustment shall then be recommended with map and description thereof to the President. The President shall advise the United States Senate and the House of Representatives of his recommendations with respect to such modification or adjustment and such recommendations shall become effective only in the same manner as provided for in subsections (b) and (c) of this section.

USE OF WILDERNESS AREAS

SECTION 4. (a) The purposes of this Act are hereby declared to be within and supplemental to the purposes for which national forests and units of the national park and wildlife refuge system are established and administered and—

(1) Nothing in this Act shall be deemed to be in interference with the purpose for which national forests are established as set forth in the Act of June 4, 1897 (30 State. 11), and the Multiple-Use Sustained-Yield Act of June 12, 1960 (74 Stat. 215).

(2) Nothing in this Act shall modify the restrictions and provisions of the Shipstead-Nolan Act (Public Law 539, Seventy-first Congress, July 10, 1930; 46 Stat. 1020), the Thye-Blatnik Act (Public Law 733, Eightieth Congress, June 22, 1948; 62 Stat. 568), and the Humphrey-Thye-Blatnik-Andersen Act (Public Law 607, Eighty-fourth

15

Congress, June 22, 1956; 70 Stat. 326), as applying to the Superior National Forest or the regulations of the Secretary of Agriculture.

(3) Nothing in this Act shall modify the statutory authority under which units of the national park system are created. Further, the designation of any area of any park, monument, or other unit of the national park system as a wilderness area pursuant to this Act shall in no manner lower the standards evolved for the use and preservation of such park, monument, or other unit of the national park system in accordance with the Act of August 25, 1916, the statutory authority under which the area was created, or any other Act of Congress which might pertain to or affect such area, including but not limited to, the Act of June 8, 1906 (34 Stat. 225; 16 U.S.C. 432 et seq.); section 3(2) of the Federal Power Act (16 U.S.C. 796 (2)); and the Act of August 21, 1935 (49 Stat. 666; 16 U.S.C. 461 et seq.).

(B) Except as otherwise provded in this Act, each agency administering any area designated as wilderness shall be responsible for preserving the wilderness character of the area and shall so administer such area for such other purposes for which it may have been established as also to preserve its wilderness character. Except as otherwise provided in this Act, wilderness areas shall be devoted to the public purposes of recreational, scenic, scientific, educational, conservation, and historical use.

PROHIBITION OF CERTAIN USES

(c) Except as specifically provided for in this Act, and subject to existing private rights, there shall be no commercial enterprise and no permanent road within any wilderness area designated by this Act and, except as necessary to meet minimum requirements for the administration of the area for the purpose of this Act (including measures required in emergencies involving the health and safety of persons within the area), there shall be no temporary road, no use of motor vehicles, motorized equipment or motorboats, no landing of aircraft, no other form of mechanical transport, and no structure or installation within any such area.

SPECIAL PROVISION

(d) The following special provisions are hearby made:

(1) Within wilderness areas designated by this Act the use of aircraft or motorboats, where these uses have already become established, may be permitted to continue subject to such restrictions as the Secretary of Agriculture deems desirable. In addition, such measures may be taken as may be necessary in the control of fire, insects, and diseases, subject to such conditions as the Secretary deems desirable.

(2) Nothing in this Act shall prevent within national forest wilderness areas any activity, including prospecting, for the purpose of gathering

16

information about mineral or other resources, if such activity is carried on in a manner compatible with the preservation of the wilderness environment. Furthermore, in accordance with such programs as the Secretary of the Interior shall develop and conduct in consultation with the Secretary of Agriculture, such areas shall be surveyed on a planned, recurring basis consistent with the concept of wilderness preservation by the Geological Survey and the Bureau of Mines to determine the mineral values, if any, that may be present; and the results of such surveys shall be made available to the public and submitted to the President and Congress.

Mineral leases, claims, etc. (3) Notwithstanding any other provisions of this Act, until midnight December 31, 1983, the United States mining laws and all laws pertaining to mineral leasing shall, to the same extent as applicable prior to the effective date of this Act, extend to those national forest lands designated by this Act as "wilderness areas"; subject, however, to such reasonable regulations governing ingress and egress as may be prescribed by the Secretary of Agriculture consistent with the use of the land for mineral location and development and exploration, drilling, and production, and use of land for transmission lines, waterlines, telephone lines, or facilities necessary in exploring, drilling, producing, mechanized ground or air equipment and restoration as near as practicable of the surface of the land disturbed in performing prospecting, location, and, in oil and gas leasing, discovery work, exploration, drilling, and production, as soon as they have served their purpose. Mining locations lying within the boundaries of said wilderness areas shall be held and used solely for mining or processing operations and uses reasonably incident thereto; and hereafter, subject to valid exisiting rights, all patents issued under the mining laws of the United States affecting national forest lands designated by this Act as wilderness areas shall convey title to the mineral deposits within the claim, together with the right to cut and use so much of the mature timber therefrom as may be needed in the extraction, removal, and beneficiation of the mineral deposits, if the timber is not otherwise reasonably available, and if the timber is cut under sound principles of forest management as defined by the national forest rules and regulations, but each such patent shall reserve to the United States all title in or to the surface of the lands and products thereof, and no use of the surface of the claim or the resources therefrom not reasonably required for carrying on mining or prospecting shall be allowed except as otherwise expressly provided in this Act: Provided, That, unless after specifically authorized, no patent within wilderness areas designated by this Act shall issue after December 31, 1983, except for the valid claims exisiting on or before December 31, 1983. Mining claims located after the effective date of this Act within the boundaries of wilderness areas designated by this Act shall create no rights in excess of those rights which may be patented under the provisions of this subsection. Mineral leases, permits, and licenses covering lands within national forest wilderness areas designated by this Act shall contain such reasonable stipulations as may be prescribed by the Secretary of Agriculture for the protection of the wilderness character of the land consistent with the use of the land for the purposes for which they are leased, permitted, or licensed. Subject to valid rights when existing, effective January 1, 1984, the minerals in lands designated by this Act as wilderness areas are withdrawn from all forms of appropriation under the mining laws and from disposition under all laws pertaining to mineral leasing and all amendments thereto.

Water resources (4) Within wilderness areas in the national forests designated by this Act, (1) the President may, within a specific area and in accordance with such regulations as he may deem desirable, authorize prospecting for water resources, the establishment and maintenance of reservoirs, water-conservation works, power projects, transmission lines, and other facilities needed in the public interest, including the road construction and maintenance essential to development and use thereof, upon his determination that such use or uses in the specific area will better serve the interests of the United States and the people thereof than will its denial; and (2) the grazing of livestock, where established prior to the effective date of this act, shall be permitted to continue subject to such reasonable regulations as are deemed necessary by the Secretary of Agriculture.

(5) Other provisions of this Act to the contrary notwithstanding, the management of the Boundary Waters Canoe Area, formerly designated as the Superior, Little Indian Sioux, and Caribou Roadless Areas, in the Superior National Forest, Minnesota, shall be in accordance with the regulations established by the Secretary of Agriculture in accordance with the general purpose of maintaining, without unnecessary restrictions on other uses, including that of timber, the primitive character of the area, particularly in the vicinity of lakes, streams and portages: Provided, That nothing in this Act shall preclude the continuance within the area of any already established use of motorboats.

(6) Commercial services may be performed within the wilderness areas designated by this Act to the extent necessary for activities which are proper for realizing the recreational or other wilderness purposes of the areas.

(7) Nothing in this Act shall constitute an express or implied claim or denial on the part of the Federal Government as to the exemption from State water laws.

(8) Nothing in this Act shall be construed as affecting the jurisdiction or responsibilities of the several States with respect to wildlife and fish in the national forests.

STATE AND PRIVATE LANDS WITHIN WILDERNESS AREAS

SECTION 5. (a) In any case where State-owned or privately owned land is completely surrounded by national forest lands within areas designated by this Act as wilderness, such State or private owner shall be given such rights as may be necessary to assure adequate access to such State-owned or privately owned land by such State or private owner and their successors in interest, or the State-owned land or privately owned land shall be exchanged for federally owned land in the same State of approximately equal value under authorities available to the Secretary of Agriculture:

Tranfers, restriction. Provided, however, That the United States shall not transfer to a State or private owner any mineral interests unless the State or private owner relinquishes or causes to be relinquished to the United States the mineral interest in the surrounded land.

(b) In any case where valid mining claims or other valid occupancies are wholly within a designated national forest wilderness area, the Secretary of Agriculture shall, by reasonable regulations consistent with the preservation of the area as wilderness, permit ingress and egress to such surrounded areas by means which have been or are being customarily enjoyed with respect to other such areas similarly situated.

Acquisition. (c) Subject to the appropriation of funds by Congress, the Secretary of Agriculture is authorized to acquire privately owned land within the perimeter of any area designated by this Act as wilderness if (1) the owner concurs in such acquisition or (2) the acquisition is specifically authorized by Congress.

GIFTS, BEQUESTS, AND CONTRIBUTIONS

SECTION 6. (a) The Secretary of Agriculture may accept gifts or bequests of land within wilderness areas designated by this Act for preservation as wilderness. The Secretary of Agriculture may also accept gifts or bequests of land adjacent to wilderness areas designated by this Act for preservation as wilderness if he has given sixty days advance notice thereof to the President of the Senate and the Speaker of the House of Representatives. Land accepted by the Secretary of Agriculture under this section shall become part of the wilderness area involved. Regulations with regard to any such land may be in accordance with such agreements, consistent with the policy of this Act, as are made at the time of such gift, or such conditions, consistent with such policy, as may be included in, and accepted with, such bequest.

(b) The Secretary of Agriculture or the Secretary of the Interior is authorized to accept private contributions and gifts to be used to further the purposes of this Act.

SECTION 7. At the opening of each session of Congress, the Secretaries of Agriculture and Interior shall jointly report to the President for transmission to Congress on the status of the wilderness system, including a list and descriptions of the areas in the system, regulations in effect, and other pertinent information, together with any recommendations they may care to make.

You may not want to dwell on each part of the Wilderness Act but rather, get an overall feel for it. A member of the Wilderness Society issued the following brief in April, 1971.

TOWARD AN UNDERSTANDING OF THE WILDERNESS ACT

The Wilderness Act as passed by the Congress on September 3, 1964 established the National Wilderness Preservation System. The preamble to the Act declares it to be "the policy of the Congress to secure for the American people of present and future generations the benefits of an enduring resource of wilderness." Elsewhere the Act states that "wilderness areas shall be devoted to the public purposes of recreational, scenic, scientific, educational, conservation, and historical use." Wilderness is not required to be "virgin," whether a forest, desert, swamp, ocean beach or other. At some time in the past it may have been logged, burned, overgrazed, lived on, even roaded, provided that at the time it is placed in the National Wilderness System any evidences of the past activities of man are, in the words of the Act, "substantially unnoticeable." There is no maximum nor minimum size limit.

Federally-owned lands on the national forests, the national parks, and the national wildlife refuges which meet the broad definition of wilderness contained in the Act may be placed in the National Wilderness System. By passage of the Act some 9,000,000 acres of national forest lands which were already being administered as wilderness by the Forest Service under its own administrative regulations went into the System. The Act establishes the procedure by which additional national forest lands may be placed in the Wilderness System and likewise qualified lands in the national park system and the national wildlife refuge system. The final step in this procedure requires passage of an act of Congress for each area added. Areas placed in the National Wilderness System continue to be a part of the same national forest, park, or wildlife refuge and administered by the same agency as before.

Just what may be done and what may not be done in an area placed in the National Wilderness Preservation System? The intent and purpose of the Wilderness Act is to assure that man does not change every acre within the United States; that some places shall be kept where nature is dominant and man comes only as a visitor — where man does not build his material things, where man does not change the face of the earth, where man does not interfere with the natural course of the waters of the earth. In short, wilderness shall be those designated places where the processes of nature continue without interference or interruption by man. It recognizes man's need for wilderness, ranging from scientific study to conservation of all forms of life, soil and water to refreshment of the human mind, body and spirit. Highly significant, wilderness assures a genetic reserve of plant and animal species which elsewhere we are altering or destroying in a wholesale way.

Within statutory wilderness the individual remains largely free to come and go and to conduct himself as he finds personally pleasing (within the usual limits of decent regard for property and for the equal rights of others). Within units of the National Wilderness System the individual retains his previous rights to enter, to camp, walk, swim, canoe, horseback, bird watch, study nature, fish and hunt (the last two subject to state and federal laws and regulations as usual). Motorized transportation of any sort is prohibited, as being inconsistent with the objectives of wilderness preservation; so that for practical purposes movement is by foot, by horse, by canoe or sailboat.

Commodity exploitation is prohibited; except that mining may be done on national forest wilderness until 1984 (an incompatible use, but one of the prices paid to get passage of wilderness legislation after an eight-year fight in the Congress). This prohibition means that there may be no logging, no drilling for oil, no mining minerals (except as noted above), no fishing nor hunting **for commercial purposes.** The agency administering the area may not manipulate the habitat, as the intent of the Act is that man shall not interfere with the normal processes of nature within the wilderness.

No works of man may be built within legal wilderness. This means that no buildings may be constructed, no power or other utility lines erected, no roads built, no dams nor reservoirs allowed. A unit of the national wilderness system is intended to be a place free of the works and the machines of man. The one exception is foot and horse trails — a recognition that most of us cannot get around even in the most magnificent wilderness without some sort of well-defined pathway.

There is a general exception to most of the above provisions with respect to the agency responsible for administering the particular wilderness area. The Wilderness Act permits the agency, insofar as it may be necessary to administer and protect the area as wilderness, to have patrol and fire roads over which agency motor vehicles only may be operated; to suppress fire, insects, and diseases; to have lookout towers and patrol cabins; and to take any measure required in an emergency for the health and safety of persons.

The Wilderness Act is not an ideal piece of legislation; nor does it pretend to establish the ideal wilderness. In the fine print of the Act are limited, special exceptions permitted under certain conditions. Certain provisions apply only to wilderness on national forests, but not in national parks and wildlife refuges. The Act represents a compromise among human beings with conflicting desires. Its intent and purpose, however, is clear: to assure that man shall have some places in this country to which he can go when seeking surcease from the noise and speed of machines, the confines of steel and concrete, the crowding of man upon man; that he or she shall have some place to go when the need is felt to be in harmony with nature and to know its peace and beauty undisturbed by man.

E.M.D.
4/30/71

CHAPTER 2
Pristine Wilderness

The wilderness purity argument conjures a claim that wilderness must be pristine, uncorrupted, fresh and clean. Pristine is a word not to be found in the Act nor in the language of the wilderness buffs. Many users are seeking "undisturbed nature." Have another look at the first paragraph of the Wilderness Act.

Part of the wilderness dilemma immediately shows up. The official labelling of an area as "National Wilderness" calls attention to the special condition of the natural terrain. Almost immediately more people appear in the area. Some complain that there are not enough trails. Others want to explore it on their ORVs. They run over signs which say "No Vehicles Beyond This Point." Word of mouth spreads the message. "The new (Green) Area is great." More people show up. The entry points may not have adequate parking. All too soon, there is a concentration of wilderness buffs. Perhaps because the trails are better in some parts, or because there is an unique lake, or possibly because some majestic cliffs make camping there more attractive than elsewhere, concentrations of hikers congregate. Consequently, as in the Pecos Wilderness, 85% of the backpackers use about 15% of the area. They love it to death. The Wilderness Managers then require permits and close some locations to overnight camping. They suggest alternatives to those wanting to camp along a stream or in a favorite meadow near a lake. The managers try to spread out the use to prevent abuse. Yet they know in so doing, they are making the inevitable collection of trash more impossible. Signs appear: "Pack it in. Pack it out." Some do; some do not.

Some wildernesses have fishable streams. Some fishermen are not careful of what they leave behind. A beer can, a worm can, some luncheon trash and even a torn wader gets tossed aside. Aluminum foil, snap tops from beverage cans, and other such trash are often left near or in a fire ring. Fires are often built near streams without any concern that the rocks become blackened. Buried trash may have been dug up by wild animals attracted by the scent. Where has the pristine environment gone?

Airplanes sometimes crash in wilderness. Each one represents a dilemma for the Regional Forester or equivalent manager in the other Public Land Agencies. Sometimes he decides to leave the wreckage there, or he specifies salvage by helicopter. If the plane was leased or rented, ownership may be hard to establish. If an insurance company can be located, various actions may follow. The Regional Forester may approve the use of power tools to disassemble the wreck for haulage out by mules. Swaths of damaged trees have been the result of snaking wrecks out of wilderness. There does not seem to be an easy, universal answer, thus the dilemma. Periodic shortage of funds in the Agency can compound the problems.

Hot air balloon crashes have started fires in wilderness. Sometimes the canopy cannot be salvaged because it is torn or enmeshed in the trees, or even partially burned. The pilot may or may not be in condition to make the next decision. He may not even know or care that he is in a Wilderness. His chase crew may not be able to get close enough to him to help. Again, there may be considerable damage done to the wilderness condition in attempts to salvage the remains. Wilderness managers may suggest that the gondola be burned and the metal parts removed from the area, with the canopy. Irreparable damage can be done without even the nearest ranger knowing about it before it is too late. No easy answer appears to fit all crashes.

Hang glider crashes are less complicated because the pieces are more portable. However, if the rescue crews are in a hurry because the pilot is hurt or it is getting dark, they have been known to penetrate Wilderness with emergency vehicles without approval. The concomitant damage to the countryside may be the least of their troubles at the time.

Motorcyclists near large cities have been known to do end runs around fences and signs to enjoy a spin in nearby Wilderness Areas. The Sandia Ranger District along the eastern city limits of Albuquerque has even installed and used instrusion detection devices to alert their patrol personnel. Unfortunately it takes another and faster cyclist to catch the miscreant. Similarly, it takes another snowmobile to intercept a violater equally mounted. A ranger on horseback is at a disadvantage unless he uses a weapon to intercept. Wheeled vehicles can damage the watershed. The snowmobile is simply excluded by the no-motorized clause in the Act. Small pine trees with tips above the snow level can be stunted and malformed by snowmobile transit. Wild animals can be frightened or otherwise disturbed by snowmobiles when they can least stand it in their weakened winter condition. An ORV law which requires a large enough license plate that the number can be read by a patrolman with binoculars has curbed violaters in some states. Rented ORVs generate a responsibility problem.

The pristine condition is consequently the wilderness manager's responsibility. He has to manage people in the wilderness, to hold back civilization. It is easy enough to say "the best way to manage wilderness is don't manage it." It is easy to say "Wilderness is the minimum budget option." However, these are only half-truths. It is more accurate to say "Manage the people in Wilderness, and do not develop the material resources." The Wilderness manager has to be sensitive to nature's values and make the decisions in the most sympathetic approach to such values.

CHAPTER 3
Initial New Mexico Wilderness Enactments

The U.S. Forest Service, after having initially opposed the Act, decided to get to work on some fifty-four wilderness areas throughout the lower forty-eight states. Five of the areas were in New Mexico. The Gila, San Pedro Parks, White Mountain, Pecos, and Wheeler Peak National Wildernesses rode the coattails of the Wilderness Act along with the other forty-nine U.S. Forest Service proposals. So the Gila National Wilderness was finally "enacted" (it had originally been only "designated") with Public Law 88-577 on September 3, 1964. The Gila Wilderness, as enacted, contained 438,626 acres.

San Pedro Parks Wilderness has a southwest corner about five miles east of Cuba, N.M. in the north central part of the state. White Mountain Wilderness is about five miles northwest of Ruidoso in the south central part of the state. The southwestern corner of the Pecos Wilderness is about seven miles northeast of Santa Fe in the north central part of the state. Wheeler Peak Wilderness is about twelve miles northeast of Taos in the northern part of the state.

The area of San Pedro Parks was 41,132 acres. White Mountain was 28,230 acres. The Pecos was 165,000 acres. The Wheeler Peak Wilderness was the smallest area (6,051 acres) of the fifty-four Forest Service areas included with the Wilderness Act. The total National Wilderness acreage in 1964 was consequently 679,039, or 1,061 square miles. Since the State of New Mexico has an area of 121,666 square miles, the one thousand plus square miles of National Wilderness was only .87%, or less than one percent of the state area. Other Rocky Mountain states and those westward had similar amounts.

The haste with which the Forest Service put together its recommendations for the areas to be enacted with the Wilderness Act made it difficult to hold separate public hearings on each area as specified in the Act. It was difficult enough to make maps that could be used for reference in the legislation. The new aerial survey maps had not been uniformly completed throughout the whole nation and some of the Forest Service Regional Offices had to resubmit their maps several times before they were considered adequate by the Anderson Senate Committee staff.[1]

Official records of the New Mexico public hearings are hard to find. However, memories of some of the old timers recall two meetings. One was in Silver City during August, 1964, but was attended by only a few agency people. There does not appear to be any newspaper item in the local papers during that month. Another public meeting was held in Santa Fe during October, 1964, after the fact. Senator Anderson was supposed to be in attendance but had to cancel for some unrecalled reason. A former National Park Service employee recalls attending the meeting but other than some of the Governor's staff, few were there, there was little public interest evident, and Senator Joseph Montoya conducted the hearing. The hearing served the purpose of making an announcement of the Act's passage and displayed a state map with the wilderness locations shown.

It is to be noted that the Pecos Wilderness was enacted (not designated) as a National Wilderness on March 11, 1955. Its area was about ten thousand acres larger at that date some eleven years before it was re-enacted in 1964 with the Wilderness Act.

Similarly the San Pedro Parks was enacted on September 16, 1940 as a Forest Service Wilderness. It, too, was re-enacted with the Act in 1964. As it was originally enacted in 1940, the area enclosed a marshy canyon bottom or a swampy mountain valley near its southwestern corner. It was referred to on some of the early maps as "el pantano." The Forest Service had an earthen dam bulldozed into the outlet in the early 1940s. The marsh became San Gregorio Lake. After passage of the Act, the lake and dam became a recognized non-conforming structure in the Wilderness Area.

Wheeler Peak Wild Area was enacted March 17, 1960, and re-enacted as a National Wilderness with the Act in 1964.

The U.S. Sports Fisheries and Wildlife Service (now named the Fish and Wildlife Service) under the Department of the Interior busily introduced some twenty areas for National Wilderness enactment consideration in 1970. The package was enacted under Public Law 91-504. It contained one area in New Mexico, the 8,500 acre Salt Creek

National Wilderness Area near Roswell at the Bitter Lake Wildlife Refuge, in the southeastern part of the state. There was a public hearing in Roswell before the enactment. Some of the hunters in the vicinity asked why it was necessary to have both a Wilderness and a Wildlife Refuge on the same ground. The answer has been lost in the passage of time, if there was one made at the hearing. When the author first visited the area in 1970, there appeared to be several trash piles from some previous activity. Four or five years later, the evidences of trash had been removed. Sandhill cranes were then grazing on the site.

The 30,850 acre Bosque del Apache Wilderness, about twelve miles south of Socorro, was enacted in 1974. It was only a part of the original Wildlife Refuge. The Sports Fisheries and Wildlife proposal was made in 1973, a public hearing was held in late 1973, and enactment was made as a matter of form in 1974. The environmental community was quite cool about the classification of the area as a Wilderness because it not only was transected by a large freeway, a railroad, a powerline, and a pipeline, it also was the location of the former Old Spanish Road, El Camino Real, and had several old Spanish ruins along the road route. The Fish and Wildlife Service claims that the Act gave their management regulations some teeth which they did not previously have.

CHAPTER 4
Public Involvement

The Wilderness Act raised the level of public awareness. It slowly became obvious to some outdoors people that the Forest Service and the Park Service would not be able to control an uneducated public in appropriate wilderness etiquette. Attitudes changed and it became apparent that the Public Land Agencies were not very enthusiastic about studying areas of the type specified in the Act. So it became the task of a few of these outdoor people to try to educate a larger sector of the public in the need for legislation to provide the primary thrust to get the Agencies moving in the Wilderness direction. The public seemed to be content to let the professionals in the public land agencies discharge the public trust. The Congress determined and inserted into the Wilderness Act a requirement for a public hearing in all Wilderness legislation events. The National Environmental Protection Act of 1969 required an EIS (Environmental Impact Statement) on each federally funded project. Such statements began to interest some parts of the public, principally the people in the outdoor recreation organizations.

Milo Conrad, an electronics technician at Sandia Laboratories in Albuquerque, had been an avid member of the New Mexico Mountain Club for many years. He had observed some of the news reports on the enactment of the Wilderness Act of 1964. During 1965 and 1966 his growing awareness, coupled with his persistence, kindled some interest in the new process of citizen involvement in public land decisions. He insisted upon the establishment of a Wilderness Committee in the Mountain Club.

A number of folks from many of the conservation organizations in Albuquerque, New Mexico, and Arizona had been joined in a loose coalition of organizations (both local and national) in a "Save Grand Canyon Committee" during the period of the major threats to the canyon. We were able to bring to bear, along with the dynamic actions of the Sierra Club, a concentrated public awareness and reaction toward a conclusion in which the dams in Marble Canyon and Hualapi Site downstream were defeated. The National Wilderness proposals had been made and the public hearings progressed through many iterations. Jeff Ingram, then the Southwest District Representative of the Sierra Club, stationed in Albuquerque, was the original coordinator pro-tem. I was elected coordinator when Jeff moved to Maine in 1967 and continued in that capacity until the committee's eventual disolution in 1971.

Dr. Bob Watt, a Los Alamos Scientific Laboratory physicist, was a river-runner and also interested in Grand Canyon's preservation. He joined our efforts as a Sierra Club representative during the peak effort. I was representing the Albuquerque and New Mexico Game Preservation Associations which were renamed the Albuquerque and New Mexico Wildlife and Preservation Associations.

In the early 1970s, the name again changed to Albuquerque Wildlife Federation. Jack Kutz was our Save Grand Canyon Committee treasurer (he was a member of the Mountain Club).

As our efforts on Grand Canyon started winding down, Milo Conrad showed up during the wilderness proposal stages. He had been to a Wilderness Society workshop in Virginia, I believe, and was able to reset our sights on New Mexico wilderness problems. Bob Watt became the chairman of the New Mexico Wilderness Study Committee, and I the co-chairman. Milo became vice-chairman, and we were off and running in 1968. Our coalition of outdoor organizations and individuals grew through the years. You will hear about its various phases in this book. The first consolidated trip by committee members made into Bandelier National Monument in July 1971 included Milo, Heister Drum, Gerry Goodman, Bill Grocke, Bart Barton, Lou Hernandez, and myself. Bandelier's eastern boundary is about fifteen miles west of Santa Fe. Many of us had been going into the Monument for years. We often touched base with the park supervisor or one of the Monument rangers, so they knew what we had in mind.

Until that time individual members of our New Mexico Wilderness Study Committee (NMWSC) had been making forays into areas which we thought were good candidates for wilderness study. A considerable part of our energy went into public education, including a concerted attempt to make the members of the outdoor groups aware of their responsibilities for the management and care of their public lands.

There were firebrands amoung us that were products of the disturbed years of the 1960s. Some of them wanted to take strong physical forcing actions against abusers of the public lands, including those people who used bulldozers to rip up and otherwise deface the defacto wilderness which we had under study. Perhaps some of these firebrands believed a bit of what they were reading in Ed Abbey's *Monkey Wrench Gang*. The educational process of the NMWSC included the teaching of the legal process towards wilderness enactment as a better alternative to violence. The endeavor appeared to be inordinately slow, but it was working. Our workshops and field trips involved us with state and federal legislators. We learned to brief Congressional candidates before they were elected on our plans for New Mexico Wilderness. We learned to work with the Congressional staff people on draft legislation. At our peak, we represented the wilderness interests of about thirty-five outdoor organizations generally through their representatives on our committee. Depending upon the specific issue, we could represent eight to ten thousand people in our outdoor organizations. We had an active newsletter and at one time mailed it to over thirteen hundred persons and organizations. Our activities were adaptations of the methods we had learned in the earlier "Save Grand Canyon" days. This time, however, we represented only New Mexico organizations.

We cut our teeth on the Bandelier Wilderness Proposal. The National Park Service was aware that the Wilderness Act specified a ten-year period for review of all of their roadless lands for wilderness consideration. Six years had already gone by and they were finally getting started.

Our Study Committee has had a number of chairmen throughout the years. For posterity they are here named and for no other reason: Bob Watt, Corry McDonald, Dave Foreman, Bob Langsenkamp, Harold Walling, Jack Kutz, Judy Bishop, Jim Stewart and Roger Peterson.

Although our membership has had representatives from the spectrum of outdoor organizations in New Mexico, a considerable number of individuals who are not generally "joiners" have come into the fold to see if they can do anything for the cause. Often they can, but generally they have to identify their own role and run with it under
our ~~~~~~~~~ r Board has to agree with the direction but it is usual-

members hate indoor meetings. Many are loners. 'h irregular meetings only for the sake of unity of action ter evokes letter responses to agency actions or congressional activities. We thrive on crises and languish in placid times.

Once a year we have what we call a "Wildervous," a wilderness rendezvous. It attempts to be a social event only and in one of our Wilderness Areas. A crisis has been known to sneak onto the agenda, but rarely. We leave no sign of our camp in such an area.

CHAPTER 5
The Wilderness versus Civilization Dichotomy

The diametric opposite of wilderness is civilization. It is considered by some as a dichotomy in which two mutually exclusive or contradictory groups of conditions stand in opposition to one another. The appurtenances of civilization are those devices of man which have intruded in wilderness, either by accident, unwittingly, or purposefully, as mentioned in Chapter 2. It is strange that one of the most civilized of man's conscious actions is restraint when it is in his best interest. Man's restraint in the (civilized) development of wilderness was finally recognized in the Wilderness Act. Man does learn slowly from cause and effect. History over the long term tends to reinforce man's cautious restraint, but not often before it is too late.[1]

Consider man's basic needs and how they interact with the environment. Man needs food and shelter. Thus he gathered seeds, berries, and animals to satisfy his primal appetite. He burned wood to keep himself warm and later for cooking. He made his shelters and furniture out of wood. Grass grew where he cut down the trees and brush. He domesticated cattle to provide a more dependable meat protein diet. He grazed cattle on the grass. He built his shelters near reliable water sources. The cattle soon overgrazed the grasses, and man had to range farther afield for wood. He planted the overgrazed fields with corn and other food crops. Soon the fields were depleted of essential minerals. He discovered that only in the flood plains of rivers and lakes that there was an annual renewal of the vital elements of fertilization. He learned a couple of tricks. One was to plant a fish with a few kernels of corn and corn would grow even in used-up soils.

Another farmer's trick was to bury his excrement in his garden. It soon decomposed and helped the soil regain some of its fertility. He learned that unless there was grass or crops in and on the soil, when it rained hard it washed away the soil. Desertification was then started. Agriculture yields less and less. The rain cycle becomes irregular. More floods devastate larger areas. A drought cycle sets in and man starves. Ethiopia is a good example.

Wilderness conditions differ considerably from the above sequence of events. The grass, brush, and trees provide a pliant bed for the acceptance of rainfall and other moisture. The watershed absorbs the water and feeds streams and springs. The trees transpire and rainfall is rejuvenated for other areas downwind. Normal forest accession, including fires and insect invasions provide new cycles of life.

As long as civilization does not interfere, wilderness provides a stable set of conditions that can survive extreme weather cycles down through the centuries. Of course a new geologic age can change all of the signals, and has, through the millennia.

Another example of the dichotomy is the rain forest. Man has obtained the essentials of life from it for thousands of years. However, in the recent century or two, man has cleared patches of rain forest, and has attempted to cultivate agricultural crops in the resulting laterite soils. He gets two or three crops and then failure. Upon abandonment, the laterite turns to a hardpan. Gully erosion soon follows and makes a wasteland of the once self-sustaining rain forest. Similar slash and burn agriculture is now common in most of the world's forests.

The Wilderness Act allows cattle grazing and some continued mining after January, 1984, if the mine was then successfully operating commercially . It also provides for the Secretary of the Interior to develop, with the Secretary of Agriculture, surveys of Wilderness Areas on a planned, recurring basis by the Geological Survey and the Bureau of Mines to determine the mineral values, if any, that may be present; and the results of such surveys shall be made available to the public and submitted to the President and Congress. Consequently, such minerals in Wilderness Areas can be made available in time of national emergencies or needs. Open pit mining in Wilderness Areas, if permitted by such a set of circumstances would obviously do irreparable damage to the natural wilderness condition. Similar damage would be caused by mineral dredging operations where large piles of rock and rubble remain for centuries. Willows and other phreatophytic trees have been known to mask such scars in old placer mining country. The remains are far from pristine wilderness.

The grazing of Wilderness Areas by cattle has been to excess in some areas. Subsequent controls by establishment of rotational pastures through fencing in the San Pedro Parks National Wilderness is a prime example. Some problems with the migration of elk have resulted. However, the controlled condition appears to be superior to the prior situation. Now, at least some unsullied use of the wilderness can be enjoyed by campers and other users in the pastures under restorations. The elk are not very vocal about their objections. Some loud bugling is to be heard but it is for another reason, in season.

Assuming that cattle grazing for human food end use is an adjunct to civilization, it is one of the few civilized uses of wilderness that is not fully a dichotomy. This is a hard point to get across to backpackers settled down for the night when a herd of cattle wanders through their camping area. Tent guy lines get pulled out occasionally. Few backpackers have guns in Wilderness except during hunting seasons. Some have to restrain themselves from shooting at such night wanderers. Curiosity may be a little understood characteristic of cattle. Horses and deer are more frequent night visitors of wilderness campsites. In some areas the half awake sleeper thinks that the visitor might be a bear.

Man, as a visitor of Wilderness, can evidence a most civilized trait of restraint by carefully not fouling his nest, by using no-impact camping practices. Yet most aspects of civilization are the anathema of Wilderness, try as hard as man might to prevent the wounding of his Wilderness.

Philosphically, mankind must consciously strive for diversity in his untrammeled landscape or everything will simmer down to a dreary sameness.[2] Initially the Wilderness Act seemed to be applicable only to high country mountain fastnesses. With the passage of the FLPMA legislation (Chapter 10), the diversity of desert wildernesses and those low country areas of public land are added where they have wilderness characteristics worth saving for posterity. The selection process goes on, hopefully before it is too late to stem the development of those lands. All potential uses must be considered by Congress before enactment. Your opinion can count. If you do not speak up, it becomes your personal dilemma.

CHAPTER 6
National Park Service Wilderness

People and civilization are nearly synonymous. The National Park Service has the task in brief:

To manage the natural areas so as to perpetuate their character and composition;

To promote and regulate appropriate park use, and seek ever to improve quality of that use; and

To provide the facilities required by the above in a manner complementing the character and special values of the area. [1]

National parks are for people to use under careful regulation. Some civilization is thus permitted to encroach upon the natural areas contained within the parks. Hardened blacktopped trails, housing structures, roads, parking lots, water development projects, and many other facilities intended to accommodate and mitigate visitors use and abuse are considered necessary.

The Wilderness Act induced the Park Service to look at park lands that might qualify as National Wilderness. Early in the process it became apparent that the Park Service employees were not enthusiastic nor could they see the necessity of having Wilderness in National Parks. Several said that such a requirement would merely lay another ply of regulations that were already too complicated to administer. That very opinion persists even today.

The public soon learned that it would require a preliminary Wilderness Proposal to induce the Park Service to hold a public hearing. Consequently the New Mexico Wilderness Study Committee (NMWSC) generated several Park Wilderness Proposals. The first was on Bandelier, the second on White Sands, and the third was on Carlsbad Caverns/Guadalupe Mountains areas. The hearings and studies resulted in the enactments on the Bandelier National Wilderness,[2] the Carlsbad Caverns National Wilderness and the Guadalupe Mountains National Wilderness,[3] but not the White Sands de facto wilderness.

The reasons why the public thought that the additional protection of National Wilderness was necessary derived from the obvious visitor centered accommodations which the Park Service seemed ever too willing to make. Proposals for tramways, for roads, signed nature trails, ranger quarters to better control visitor misuse of special park features, all alerted a growing public awareness of an overeager administration. We could almost foresee a public encapsulated in a number of closed vehicles saying "look but do not touch." The park wilderness areas were worth classifying as National Wilderness for their own values.

The Park Service was quick to pick up the significance of the statement in the Wilderness Act which provides, in part, that:

... the designation of any area of park ... as a Wilderness Area pursuant to this Act shall in no manner lower the standards evolved for the use and preservation of such park ... in accordance with the Act of Aug. 25, 1916, (and) the statutory authority under which the area was created. ....[4]

The Park Service does not allow cattle grazing, game animal hunting, mineral prospecting, water conservation, and power projects. There are some notable exceptions but they are not widespread. There have been a few grazing permits on the north side of Grand Canyon adjacent to some private inholdings or there have been infrequent efforts to control grazing there. The area is quite far from a ranger's reach. There may not have been game animal hunting but the use of guns has been endorsed in the attempted control of burro overpopulation in some of the parks. There is continuing uranium mining going on within a mile of Grand Canyon Village. There have been two attempts to put in dams for power generation in the Grand Canyon National Park. The Park Service maintained a low profile during the public outcry possibly because the Department of Interior and the U.S. Army Engineers were involved in the dam site surveys. Actually, the dam sites were just outside the park boundaries, but they would have had telling effects on the park.

The Park Service has allowed the use of helicopters in Grand Canyon Wilderness for hauling construction material (I was close by when it happened near Phantom Ranch), for fire and insect disease control, rescue, transplanting excess animals to other locations, and for archaeological party support. They are currently attempting to regulate the commercial flights into the Canyon gorge as well as over the adjacent Wilderness Areas. The Canyon attracts such an overload of visitation that controlling all of the misuse is next to impossible. A different kind of accident occurs almost daily. Luckily, not many of them are in the National Wilderness Area near the park. Much of the public and many of the park's summer employees do not know where some of the boundaries are.

There have been attempts made to completely unify the wilderness management and administration regulations among the Forest Service, the Park Service, Fish and Wildlife Service, and the Bureau of Land Management. One view holds that all of the basic provisions are the same but that each agency has its own unique problems and dilemmas to satisfy. The diametric view insists that there can be no completely common ground for all agencies responsible for National Wilderness. Many of us stand in the middle of such extremes. As new threats appear, why lose the opportunity to be uniform in response? The mountain bicycles are a good example. The rangers seem to take widely varying approaches. Perhaps because not enough clear language is used on access point signs, the public can claim ignorance. A couple of instances have come to our attention where the ranger insisted on the bicycle being carried out and then later compromised in its being pushed out riderless.

All told it is difficult for both the public and the Park Service field personnel to understand all of the nuances of managing wilderness inside of National Parks. Some people cannot understand the differing grades of parkland categories such as Wilderness, Monument, Administrative Area, etc. When they cannot even read and interpret signs, the dilemma deepens.

CHAPTER 7
U.S. Forest Service and the Roadless Area Review and Evaluation Process in New Mexico

The Forest Service had been looking wonderingly at the Wilderness Act requirements without any definitive action. They were hard put to do the job of managing the National Forests without any extra work piled onto their tasks. They had been kind of burned out on wilderness by the work of complying with the original enactments of the Wilderness Act. So six years of the ten went by. Finally, in mid 1971, they decided that they must start the review process. They had decided earlier that each Ranger District could not do the job without some guidelines. They eased into the task by setting up an inter-disciplinary team out of many western regions. The Forest Service had done a commendable job of cataloging and recommending the 54 areas which they chose to accompany the Wilderness Act in 1964. Those people that had been through that somewhat galling process were not very anxious to start again. They heard some of the public saying emphatically "We have too much wilderness now." For some of the rangers already overloaded by paperwork, the whole deal was a paradox. For the public it was an enigma, hard to understand and do.

In March 1972, William D. Hurst, Regional Forester of our southwest region, issued a document 2310 (2100) disclosing a summary of the inventory made by the interdisciplinary team. We, the NMWSC, had been talking to the rangers and Forest Service supervisors in New Mexico forest offices for at least a couple of years prior to 1972. Many of our recommendations and opinions were contained in the details of the inventory, but the listed areas appeared to be short of our recommendations. A list of public meetings was included and public opinions to be expressed therein were to be received by each Forest Supervisor by June 10, 1972.

A consolidated report was made to the Chief of the Forest Service by each Regional Forester by year's end. In October, 1973, a (RARE) Roadless Area Review and Evaluation Report No. 11 was submitted to the Congress. It also said that a final Environmental Statement on New Wilderness Study Areas was filed with the President's Council on Environmental Quality in October 1973. So the U.S. Forest Service and the Secretary of Agriculture made their "Chief's List" report within the time limits specified in the Act.

The NMWSC (Wilderness Study Committee) had been submitting draft Wilderness Bills on the New Mexico areas on which we had concentrated. We had done our field work and submitted maps to our congressmen with supportive pictures and other information in response to purported conflicts. Our areas included some that were not on the Chief's List, and others that were generally larger than those "studied" by the Forest Service. It became evident that there was a strong purist strain in the Forest Service selections and that they were applying an impairment doctrine that was far more stringent than ours. For example, an occasional stump remaining from some previous wood-gathering activity would be found to be the disqualifying factor between our boundary marking and theirs. They were also inclined to make the corridor of access along a road much wider than ours.

When the ten-year anniversary of the Wilderness Act came and went without any legislation on New Mexico Wilderness Areas, we were a bit disconsolate in the Study Committee. We did continue to work on the areas on our priority lists and to prepare maps. Workshops and field trips were continued and continuing dialogues with our congressmen's staffs were normal. In 1975 we pulled together a proposed New Mexico Omnibus Wilderness Bill and put it in all of the appropriate hands in Washington, D.C.

The paucity of coordinated legislative action deriving from the earlier RARE I review made it an election issue in 1976. Presidential candidate Carter was briefed beforehand and the entire environmental issue had some bearing on his being elected in 1976. The change of administration soon sent out signals of renewed hope to us.

Since there had been an earlier RARE activity, a second one became RARE II as it progressed. The new Assistant Secretary of Agriculture, Rupert Cutler, made it known that a systematic and concentrated process of review and evaluation of National Forest lands was being started. The old line foresters were jolted both in the administrative priorities given wilderness and the subsequent analytical methodologies interjected into the RARE processes. A unified scoring system was set up among other things including some policy changes relating to wilderness purity. These purity criteria came closer to our NMWSC opinions than the RARE I standards did. We had to learn a new methodology of evaluation and began to sympathize with the Forest Service staffers whom we knew quite well. The NMWSC Workshops increased in number and intensity and so did the public meetings called by the Forest Service. These were often two or more per week in different parts of the state, each going over their local areas and issues.

A National Summary of Public Comments on the RARE II Inventory and Evaluation Criteria was issued in November 1977. Statistical charts indicated a growing alertness of the public to wilderness matters but public apathy was given some measure for the first time. Public education on wilderness concepts had always been difficult. The new administration possibly was too far ahead of the public and its legislative representatives. We in the NMWSC had to alert our Senators and Representatives on many of these changes in thinking and to demonstrate the public support of the new look. Newspaper and magazines articles, letters, and news releases including TV coverage all played their parts. Many of these were not easy to generate.

Our successes with Bandelier, Chama River, Sandia and Manzano Mountains National Wilderness enactments encouraged us with the workability of the legal process. The discouragements with the RARE I and II Forest Service periods were reconciled as only minor perturbations of the process. The RARE II Forest Service recommendations were made on January 4, 1979, and contained far less than we had recommended and supported with so many thousands of letters and petitions. The public hearings, listening sessions, and unofficial meetings seemed endless. We tried to be consistent and moderate throughout the many years involved.

The following chart encapsulates the RARE II recommendations made by the Forest Service versus our New Mexico Wilderness Study Committee Proposals:

Carson National Forest	**Acres Recommended**	
Area	**Our Proposal**	**Forest Service**
Latir Peak	26,500	24,600 W
Wheeler Peak Additions	17,000	14,700 W

| | Acres Recommended | |
Area	Our Proposal	Forest Service
Pecos Additions	20,000*	13,000 W
Columbine-Hondo (Gold Hill)	50,500	46,050 FP
Osier Mesa-Cruces Basin	32,600	NW
Canjilon-El Rito	19,800	NW
Sierra Negra	16,400	NW
Bull Canyon	12,200	NW

*(See Santa Fe N.F. Pecos Adds. for Total)

Santa Fe National Forest

Pecos Wilderness Additions	154,500	71,00 W; 17,530 FP
Dome	5,200	W
Caja	14,000	NW
Polvadera Peak	15,480	FP
Caballo Mountain	8,800	FP
Peralta Canyon	13,400	NW
Chama Canyon Adds.	4,800	FP
San Pedro Parks Adds.	5,670	FP
Canones Pedernal	12,900	NW
Corral	11,000	NW
Virgin	6,250	NW

Cibola National Forest

Banco Breaks	12,650	NW
Apache Kid	99,182	133,00 W
Canadian River	4,020	4,020 W
Withington	19,000	19,000 W
Ryan Hill	45,000	36,640 FP
Scott Mesa	40,000	NW
Mt. Taylor	6,360	NW
San Jose	17,890	NW
White Cap	11,800	NW
Ranger Cabin	6,380	NW
Cerro Alesna	6,910	NW

Lincoln National Forest

Capitan	38,000	36,400 W
Southern Guadalupes	21,300	21,000 W
White Mountain Wilderness Adds.	20,560	19,600 W
Little Dog & Pup	25,920	FP
North Rocky Canyon	6,810	NW
Carrizo Peak	16,450	NW
Last Chance Canyon	9,860	NW
Ortega	10,890	NW

Coronado National Forest

Whitmire Canyon	18,000	12,740 FP
Bunk Robinson	15,850	FP

Gila National Forest

Aldo Leopold	315,000	251,000 W
Gila Wilderness Additions	228,137	163,968 W
Blue Range	40,000	40,000 W
San Francisco	19,000	8,800 W
Hell Hole	18,860	FP
Gila Middle Box	32,000	NW
Devil's Creek	91,000	NW
Frisco Box	40,000	NW
Sawyers Peak	64,200	NW
Aspen Mountain	22,100	NW
T-Bar	7,000	NW
Nolan	18,840	NW
Mother Hubbard	6,500	NW

W = Wilderness   NW = Non-wilderness   FP = Further Planning

Alternatives Considered in RARE II

The Forest Service categorized a number of alternatives (A through J) in doing their final Environmental Statement:

Alternative A: No other action than that presently being followed in land and resource management planning would take place, with activities continuing as if RARE II did not exist.

Alternative B: All roadless areas are allocated to non-wilderness uses.

Alternative C: Emphasis is on high resource outputs, but consideration is given areas rated high in wilderness attributes.

Alternative D: Emphasis is given areas with high wilderness attributes, but any of those areas with significant resource production potential are placed in the further planning category.

Alternative E: Emphasis is on achieving an established minimum level representation of landform, ecosystem, associated wildlife, and accessibility characteristics in the Wilderness System.

Alternative F: Emphasis is on achieving an established moderate level of the same characteristics as Alternative E in the Wilderness System.

Alternative G: Emphasis is on achieving an established high-level of the same characteristics as Alternative E in the Wilderness System.

Alternative H: Emphasis is on allocation of roadless areas on the basis of regional and local needs, as perceived by the Forest Service.

Alternative I: Emphasis is on adding areas with the highest wilderness attributes to the Wilderness System, with secondary consideration being given to areas of high resource production potential.

Alternative J: All roadless areas are recommended for wilderness.

They then selected a "combination of Alternatives C and I, modified in response to public comment received on the draft environmental statement, existing laws and regulations, identified public needs, and professional judgement by Department of Agriculture decisionmakers."

When we saw the RARE II Recommendations made by the Forest Service in accordance with their final alternative, the New Mexico Wilderness Study Committee countered with our own Alternative W. The poker game began in earnest. Our Alternative W totaled 1,792,469 acres, or 2.3% of the area of New Mexico. The Forest Service's RARE II Recommendations totaled 825,288 acres of Wilderness and 208,340 acres for Further Planning.

The next part of the legal process was evident on April 17, 1979, when President Carter made the Administration's recommendation to Congress. It essentially followed the Forest Service's prescription in New Mexico except that it added 7,800 acres to the 8,800 acre area of the lower San Francisco Canyon in the Gila National Forest. However, it changed the Forest Service's recommended Further Planning category for the Banco Breaks and relegated it to Non-Wilderness use. The changes resulted from the Office of Management and Budget's review of the Forest Service's reports.

The wheels of misfortune really started to turn. External events began to mold opinions and militate against normal wilderness legislative actions.

Secretary of Interior Andrus signed an order to withdraw 40 million acres of wildlife refuge in Alaska to restrain some threatening developments in the area. Not only did this irritate many of the people in Alaska, but it caused much of the growing animosity between the Administration and the Congress. Congress has guarded its prerogative to make such public land decisions, and had specified the processes in the Wilderness Act and in the Federal Land Planning and Management Act (FLPMA), among others (see Chapter 10).

Other events had different impacts on the national scene, as if these already described were not enough. Other states had similar reactions to ours to the RARE II pronouncements, and some read things differently. For example, the state of California initiated a suit against the Department of Agriculture in July, 1979, in which it was claimed that the Forest Service failed to comply with the requirements of the National Environmental Policy Act in designating California roadless areas as non-wilderness under the RARE II program. The Federal District Court made its ruling on January 8, 1980, barring development on forty-seven roadless areas in California until the environmental impact statements are prepared for the areas in question. Of course the land developers in our most populous state became very vocal against wilderness and castigated the multiple-use of our forests.

Our opinion is that as long as there had been no congressional action, the public is enjoined from development of all of the roadless areas until some kind of resolution of the RARE process is completed.

Meanwhile, Congress claimed to have waited patiently for the Administration to produce a draft bill to wrap-up the RARE process. The individual state delegations decided that they could wait no longer and invited the public input for various kinds of wilderness bills applying to their states. On December 6, 1979, eleven months after the Forest Service had made its RARE II recommendations, the New Mexico Delegation invited the public to help "prepare a bill that would create wilderness areas on Forest Service lands in the state," (*Albuquerque Journal*, page A-8, December 6, 1979).

Our NMWSC had been at work for several months getting our final recommendations ready for such an occasion. The poker game resumed in earnest. We made our bid with our Alternative W, including the fifty-two areas named in the list earlier in this chapter. True, we did not expect to get anything like the whole list. The Forest Service had added some areas to their RARE I list of 1972 when they made their subsequent RARE II list. After looking at those surprise additions, several looked like they might have been included to provide sacrifice chips in the Chief's final list. Conversely, our bottom line was the Forest Service's RARE II list, as much as we thought it was too skimpy.

So we provided our Senators and Representatives with maps and descriptions of each area that we particularly wanted, 8x10-inch color prints of good slides of each area were also furnished for the hearings. It is disconcerting to have to rely on the judgments of people that have never seen the areas which are being considered. It is difficult, if not impossible, to sufficiently describe a wilderness to a person that does not have the frame of reference for it. The delegation can only attempt to balance the pressures between the developers and the environmentalists. The developers can hold out the promise of more jobs and a "healthier economic climate." The outdoor people can talk about the beauty of the status quo instead of the quid pro quo.

Another event was interjected into the growing maelstrom, and it proved to have disturbing effects. Representative Thomas Foley (D.-Washington) introduced legislation in January, 1980, to instantly commit to permanent non-wilderness status all thirty-six million acres recommended for non-wilderness by the Forest Service. It also stipulated that areas recommended for wilderness but not designated by January 1, 1984, would automatically lapse into non-wilderness status. (Wilderness Report, Vol 17, No. 1; The Wilderness Society.)

Then, in March, 1980, Rep. Foley dropped the other boot. It came in the guise of a pro-wilderness measure, since it ratified all of the Administration's RARE II wilderness recommendations. But then it went on about releasing the other 36 million acres for uses other than wilderness. Isn't that tempting? If you are tired and weary of the battle, why should you hold out for Utopia? We cannot be that tired, ever.

Our national economy was not in the best of condition during this whole period. Our trade balances had been adversely affected by the necessity of importing not only petroleum products but a growing list of critical minerals. No one felt or understood this vital situation more keenly than our Senator Schmitt, our astronaut geologist. Our Representative Runnels, being in the oil business, was also very sensitive to our state's oil and gas resources. Consequently, any roadless area that has even the slightest hint of mineral resources of any kind in our state was of abiding interest to one or both of these genetlemen.

The legal process can get complicated by the interplay of these many factors and events. Add to these some influences of inflation and budgeting restrictions, and it is a wonder that any Federal action can take place. One recent example (in June, 1980) was evident in the fact that even after the President had signed the bill to acquire and enact the Elena Gallegos tract into the Sandia Mountain Wilderness, it required a separate appropriation of $20 million to accomplish the fact (see Chapter 11).

The New Mexico Wilderness Act of 1980 was issued for comment by our delegation on April 15, 1980. It included approximately 560,400 acres as Wilderness, designated 26,000 acres of the "San Francisco Wilderness Area Proposed" to further study, and released the remaining RARE II Forest Service Areas to non-wilderness use. This draft legislation was at least 300,000 acres under our bottom line. It completely left out our favorite Apache Kid Area.

We were assured by our delegation that the bill was negotiable and that we had until May 15, 1980, for comments. When we tried to find out which parts of areas were omitted and why, we were told that maps had been sent to their local offices by facsimile. The quality of the maps, which were crude to begin with, did not improve in the electronic transmission. When we did get some legible maps in the mail, we met with a stonewall on the questions of omission. The aides to the delegation said that the principals did not want to be put on the defensive for their recommendations in the draft bill.

You can understand why we began to feel that our world had come apart. We asked for an extension on the comment date to May

46

28, 1980, and were granted it. We paid several thousands of donated dollars to place large ads in the Albuquerque, Santa Fe, and Las Cruces newspapers asking that the public react to the draft bill. This was one time that both the pro- and anti-wilderness forces were of one mind, to stop the bill.

Our NMWSC representatives went to Washington to testify on May 28, 1980. Jim Stewart, Dave Foreman, George Grossman, and LeBron Hardy presented our case well. Others of us submitted written statements for the Congressional Record. There was very little endorsement of the proposed bill by any of the groups represented except one by the state of New Mexico. (Our then Governor even went on record for the Sagebrush Rebellion tenets.) Only the two Senators were able to attend their own hearing. There followed a deep silence of two weeks.

Congressional aides started to call our chairman with proposed revisions of the areas to be included in a marked-up bill. They even conceded a 60,000 acre Apache Kid Wilderness and made entree of other concessions. Our reaction was that, as long as the release language was contained in the bill, we could not negotiate revisions of the wilderness areas for inclusion. It was implied that the Colorado bill was undergoing mark-up and that its release language could be substituted for that in our bill. The specifics of that revised Colorado bill's language were not available, so negotiations stopped again. A rumor had it that the Colorado draft bill had an extension of the December 31, 1983 date of closure of permitted mining in wilderness areas to the year 2000. Open pit mining would be permitted. Congress again seemed to want its cake and eat it too.

Our new NMWSC chairman, Harold Walling, called the Congressmen and asked that he be advised of any further proposed changes as they were offered. My own written testimony as a director of our committee offers to assist with a release list of areas we possibly could agree upon on the condition that it would not compromise or hazard the legal processes in other states as well as ours. The last word we had on the bill's status was that it was too late to mark it up before the summer recess of the Session.

Some of us felt that the whole RARE II process was abortive. We never had liked the necessity of dealing with multiple enactments because we have limited resources to bring together all of the current information pertinent to the entire public land legislative package. We think that the original intent of the Wilderness Act was that each area be studied individually, analyzed, and evaluated. Then, if several areas are ready for simultaneous enactment, a small omnibus bill could result appropriately. It is difficult to have confidence that a bill with eleven pieces of wilderness in the same National Forest Region can be well constituted.

Enactment of Capitan Mountain (36,400 acres), White Mountain Additions (19,000 acres), Dome (5,200 acres), and Withington (19,000 acres) as a package without any release language would be reasonable. Even an environmental impact statement on those areas would be credulous. These areas were included in the nefarious New Mexico Wilderness Act of 1980 which had been stalled.

Looking at the seven other areas also contained in that "anti-wilderness" bill, North McKittrick Canyon was left out of the Guadalupe Escarpment (18,000 acres) on the supposition that there may be a small oil deposit therein. It is going to be expensive to find out. The Pecos Additions (70,000 acres) contains less than half of the qualified lands in them. Latir Peak (15,600 acres) is ten thousand acres short of the fact because of faulty information analyses. Wheeler Peak Additions (9,100 acres) is slightly more than half of the qualified lands surrounding the small Wilderness Area. The Aldo Leopold (178,000 acres) and Gila Additions (155,000 acres) are just arbitrary decisions being only half of the qualified areas. The reduction of the Blue Range (35,000 acres) from 40,000 is unconscionable bean-counting.

As the summer of 1980 rolled on, nothing happened in Washington to the ill-fated draft wilderness bill until Congressman Harold Runnels died without leaving any final instructions. This left the vacancy in District II and delayed hearings in the House. The Colorado bill shaped up into a fairly palatable piece of legislation. This induced several letters of thanks and commendations to Colorado Senators Hart and Armstrong from many of us that occasionally use some of the wilderness areas.

Governor King did not call a specific election or otherwise manage to make an appointment to fill the late Congressman's seat. The newspapers reported a great deal of jockeying for position. The Governor's nephew, David King, changed his residency to be within the Second District's boundaries and was placed on the ballot. Mrs. Harold Runnels attempted to file for the position but was disqualified on some technicality which was not clearly reported in the media. The Republican Party did not have a Congressional candidate for the Second District in the primary election and was thus disqualified from having one in the 1980 November national elections. Joe Skeen, a sheepman from the Second District, had run for Governor as a Republican but had been defeated by previous Democratic endeavors. Skeen appealed the disqualification process in a U.S. District court in

Denver and was on the November ballot.

Meanwhile, in District One, Bill Richardson won a bid for Congressman in the primary election and became the Democratic candidate competing for Congressman Manuel Lujan's (R) seat. Our Wilderness Study Committee briefs all new candidates on the public land issues impinging upon wilderness and its enactment, so we tried to brief David King at the same time we were talking to Bill Richardson, since King was on the November ballot in the Second District. He had been a friend in the past and does know a great deal about the public land issues in the state already. However, he did not appear at our briefing.

In September, the New Mexico delegation maneuvered to attach their wilderness bill to the cleared Colorado bill which was ready to be sent to the House. They were able to put a hold on the Colorado bill. The Colorado Senators argued that the House Public Lands Subcommittee might scuttle the entire the bill, including the Colorado portion, if the New Mexico bill were added to the legislation.

Our Senators Domenici and Schmitt (both R.) then released their hold on the Colorado bill after Senator Dale Bumpers (D. - Ark.), Chairman of the Senate Public Lands Subcommittee, agreed to bring the New Mexico bill to the Senate floor as quickly as possible, and if the House Interior Committee would promise hearings after the November elections (Lame Duck Session).

The next piece of the legal process jigsaw puzzle came in by telephone to our new chairman, Harold Walling, from the Washington delegation offices. His letter of September 24, 1980 said that the foregoing actions led to the following scenario:

1. *If President Carter is re-elected, kill the bill and subsequently work up an improvement for passage next year.*

2. *If Governor Reagan is elected, settle quickly for the best combination we can get while Carter is in office; anticipate no subsequent enactments.*

3. *Continue to work on release language moderation.*

4. *Expect a pro-development replacement of the deceased Representative Runnels. Settle quickly if Richardson is not elected.*

5. *Anticipate a pre-election briefing of the new candidates for the pending third congressional seat.*

6. *Senator Domenici will introduce the bill to the Senate; Senator Schmitt will endorse it. Representative Lujan will sponsor it in the House Committee. A joint resolution will evolve via Representative Seiberling.*

We had a hint that the release language applied only to the RARE II Areas in the Gila and Aldo Leopold vicinities. Until we had a copy of the proposed bill, we could not react in any rational way. Our chairman had shown that he rapidly learned the rules of the game. His letter lists the areas in the proposed bill:

Aldo Leopold, 211,300 acres; 100 k less than our proposed area, and 40 k less than RARE II.

Gila Additions, 130,300 acres; 110 k less than our proposed areas, and 34 k less than RARE II.

Blue Range, 30,000 acres; one half of our proposed area. 10 k more than RARE II.

San Francisco, 25,600 acres for "Further Study."

Pecos Addiitions, 70,730 acres; about half of our proposed and equal to RARE II.

Wheeler Peak, 9,100 acres; half of our proposal, and less than 15,200 RARE II.

Latir, 24,000 acres; about 2200 acres less than our proposal and 2000 less than RARE II.

Apache Kid, 40,000 acres; only 40% of our proposal and 90 k less than RARE II. This is a real mistake. Core area is too far north.

Withington, 19,000 acres; larger than our proposal by 700 acres, and rounded down from RARE II by about 100 acres.

Capitan, 34,000 acres; 6 k less than our proposal and 2.5 k less than RARE II.

White Mountain Additions, 16,800 acres; 5 k less than ours, and 4 k less than RARE II.

As it stood before amendment, Dome and Guadalupe Escarpment were not included. The Guads were omitted probably because they are in the vicinity of Harold Runnel's territory. Why the Dome was left out is unknown. One can guess that the Park Service was cool to the possibilities of "managing" a partially burned area along with Bandelier.

If everything else in RARE II were to be released to non-wilderness uses, we probably would not be placated. Most of the areas included in the above (most recent) tabulation may be hard to manage because of the fragments remaining outside of the Wilderness Areas. This results from the bargaining process and mapping by people unfamiliar with the land in question. The Forest Service may be able to better locate the boundaries when they lay out the legal boundaries.

Our annual Wilderness Rendezvous (Wildervous) was planned for mid-October 1980 on the ridge south of Capilla Peak in the Manzano Mountain Wilderness. Hopefully we would know the final details of the legislation at that time. We suspected that, if Reagan were elected President, the final bill would not be signed because of his avowed "state's rights" position.

The legislative process is endless, or so it seems. But you, too, can play the game if you think the stakes are worth the effort. Many of us have worked a dozen years to provide you the base for continuing.

Another piece of the puzzle fell into place in the first few days of October, 1980. Senator Domenici introduced a bill to reimburse a Rodriguez family in the amount of $24,000 for land and a house in the area subsequently determined to be Taos Pueblo land. Then he attached our delegation's RARE II bill to that private bill. Again, we were unable to obtain a copy but the news article reports that "all RARE II lands not included in the bill (are released) from further consideration for wilderness status, then makes the land available for multiple use." The Senate passed the bill on September 30, 1980. On October 2, 1980, the bill was tabled for the election recess and would be opened again "when the Congress comes back to finish its work in the Lame Duck Session starting November 12," after the National Election. Those congressmen not re-elected pay only casual attention to many matters of considerable importance during such sessions.

We tried to find a basis for defeating the release language in that the Wilderness Act takes precedence and requires careful individual determination of each roadless area's destiny.

The November election results were surprising, in that Governor Reagan won the Presidency, Representative Lujan narrowly defeated Bill Richardson, and Joe Skeen beat David King in a successful write-in ballot on the southern district. Thus, there was a complete Republican sweep of the New Mexico seats.

Joe Skeen told our Committee several years ago when we were briefing him on the wilderness issues (prior to his unsuccessful bid for the governorship against Bruce King) that he "knows all about our Wildernesses." He indicated that he had flown his National Guard jets up all of the canyons every weekend for years. We commented that such activities may not be legal processes.

Representative John Seiberling (D.- Ohio) appeared on the scene on November 7, 1980, in Santa Fe and Albuquerque. He was the chairman of the Public Lands Subcommittee of the House Interior and Insular Affairs Committee. Senator Domenici had been announced as the new Senate Budget Committee Chairman under the new Administration. Having been on that Committee for several years, the election elevated him as the ranking majority party member. That sudden shift in the wind kept him from attending, with the rest of the delegation, an inspection trip of our proposed Wilderness.

So they swept into the scene with little fanfare. Chairman Seiberling's staff, led by an Andy Weissner, and a Jim Huska quietly arranged several sorties and landings at various refueling sites near key locations to meet with the various users of the public lands in question. Senator Schmitt and Representative Lujan were in the tour party. Gene Hassell, the Regional Forester, and his staff arranged and furnished three helicopters to transport the group through all of the mountain chains involved.

We met the delegation at Tres Piedras, near San Cristobal, at Truchas, at a heliport near the Apache Kid, and at several other places where they refueled. We had our various key honchos, armed with our maps and first-hand knowledge of the contested boundaries, at each stop. The local ranchers, the timber operators, and the miners all represented their views. At Tres Piedras I brashly welcomed the Colorado Grazing permitees on the Carson National Forest to our New Mexico Wilderness Areas so our delegation would know "where their votes were coming from." The only hint of trouble surfaced at Truchas when a young firebrand representing the land grant interests became embroiled in arguments with timbermen and conservationists just before the choppers landed. Luckily, no knives had been drawn. Congressman Manuel Lujan soothed the situation and Chairman Seiberling rerouted the subjects. Although obviously pro-wilderness, Seiberling was objectively fair and considered all interests.

One undertone bubbled quietly in the background. A strong rumor that Lujan would be appointed Secretary of Interior under the Reagan administration surfaced in several forms.

Another nuance of the legal process is that the Democrat (Bill Richardson) ran such a strong race against Lujan, if Manuel were appointed Secretary, Richardson could possibly swing the subsequent special election. That fact could make Reagan appoint another candidate than Lujan so the House seat would not be lost to the Democrats. Richardson responded to our pre-election briefing quite favorably. If Manuel were to become Secretary of Interior, however, he could be in for a rough time with the ebbing tide of the Sagebrush Rebellion, and the strong states' rights stand of the new administration. Our next protracted battle was anticipated to be the BLM Wilderness sequence under FLPMA (Federal Land Planning Management Act) (see Chapter 10).

The closure of our omnibus bill was expected to come out of some modification in boundaries generated by the chopper tour, by some judicious changes in release language which had been suggested, by compromising more than all parties wanted to, and by pulling hard down the last leg to the finish line. The time frame was limited to the next month before the end of the session. Our delegation was anxious to close the issue without making everyone exasperated. I am trying to report it as coolly as I can, though I am far from capable of giving you a detached account.

The *Albuquerque Journal* of November 22, 1980, carried an AP artical headlined, "Lujan's Wilderness Plan Wins Approval of House." It mentioned a figure of 609,000 acres. Many of the areas appeared to be adjusted upwards in size.

The Senate version was within minutes of passage on November 25 when the Senate unexpectedly recessed until December 1. Some of us conjured a number of fanciful suppositions of how the opposition might pull a hat trick. The Senate did pass their bill on December 1. Some of the figures differed between the two bills.

By chance, I was in Washington on December 4th and 5th on other matters. I inquired about the possibility of witnessing the signing of the bill by the President. That proved to be impossible because the reconciled bill was not put on the executive desk until December 10. I wanted a wilderness pen to finish my book.

Again, we started to worry anew. We could guess that the President would be beset with half-truths which could be hard to confirm or refute by a lame duck staff. He may have been badgered by many such problems, and he was surely bothered by renewals of the hostage crisis, but he finally signed our New Mexico Wilderness Act of 1980 (Public Law 96-550) amended on December 19, 1980. We had fears of having to wait for four years until another window of opportunity could open again.

The 1980 Christmas Holidays made it difficult to get a copy of the actual act as the President signed it. The official acreage is listed here for posterity:

1.	Aldo Leopold	211,300	7.	Apache Kid	45,000
2.	Gila Additions	140,000	8.	Withington	19,000
3.	Blue Range	30,000	8.	Capitan	34,000
4.	Pecos Additions	55,000	10.	White Mount. Adds.	16,860
5.	Wheeler Pk. Adds.	14,700	11.	Dome (Bandelier Adds.)	5,200
6.	Latir	20,000	12.	Cruces Basin	18,000
					609,060

The locations of those areas not previously given are described here to aid in finding them. The Aldo Leopold Wilderness is immediately to the east of the Gila Mountains, encompassing the Black Range. The Blue Range Wilderness is about 12 miles northwest of the

Gila Wilderness and straddles the Arizona-New Mexico border. The Latir Wilderness is in the Sangre de Cristo Mountains about 12 miles north of Mount Wheeler near the northern state border. The Cruces Basin Wilderness is about 50 miles west of Latir along the border. The Apache Kid Wilderness is about 40 miles southwest of Socorro in the southwestern part of the state. The Withington Wilderness is about seven miles north of the Apache Kid Wilderness, and approximately 30 miles from Socorro. The Capitan Wilderness is about 25 miles east of Carrizozo in the south central part of the state.

The act included six areas for Further Study until January 1, 1986. They are: Lower San Francisco Wilderness Study Area, Guadalupe Escarpment WSA, Bunk Robinson WSA, Columbine-Hondo WSA, Hell Hole WSA, and Whitmire Canyon WSA. Lower San Francisco and Hell Hole WSAs are along the Arizona border west the Gila. Bunk Robinson and Whitmire Canyon are in the very southwestern corner of the state. The Guadalupe Escarpment WSA is the Forest Service area between Carlsbad and Guadalupe Mountain National Park in the southeastern part of the state. The Columbine-Hondo WSA is between Wheeler Peak and Latir Wilderness Areas.

The release language was toned down to say that all other areas reviewed in RARE II did not require further review for wilderness options, and that they could be managed in accord with the Forest and Rangeland Renewable Planning Act of 1974 and the National Forest Management Act of 1976. Consequently, we did not interpret this to mean that the omitted lands would be turned loose to unbridled development or abuse. Our continued access to reason is through participation in the public process with the Forest Service planning activities.

The Act did include several other features: a 31,000 acre Langmuir Research Site (our Ryan Hill WSA 14 miles west of Socorro) was enacted to continue access of the lightning lab; a Chaco Culture Natural Historical park of 33,900 acres 70 miles north of Grants in the northwest part of the state; and a Salinas National Monument to include old Abo, Quarai, and Gran Quivira village sites to the east and southeast of our Manzano Mountain Wilderness. Mr. Seiberling, and other members of the Committee on Interior and Insular Affairs managed to negotiate a compromise which added our Cruces Basin and other increases to a total area of 24,300 acres more than the replaced version. The figures appear to bear a great similarity to the original Domenici bill.

One might conclude that it is now time to sit back and contemplate what could have happened, but the legislative process does not stop here. The Act goes on to say that the Secretary of Agriculture (Forest Service) shall file maps referred to in this Act and legal (boundary) descriptions of each designated wilderness area, as soon as practicable. The maps referred to in the Act are less than a cartographer's dream. The scale is inadequate, the boundaries are broad brush and even the areas were best guesses. They are the starting point.

Even so, this allows a considerable amount of judgment in the establishment of the legal boundary. You are urged to get in touch with the chief honcho for each area and help him work with the appropriate Forest Ranger to get the task done. Although the honchos change from time to time, our New Mexico Wilderness Study Committee can always put you in touch with the right honcho for each area. Continuing oversight of the management of his chosen area is his labor of love.

Possibly you would prefer to adopt a wilderness study area on or off the list in the Act for your attention. The Study Committee can help you get started. The roadless area review process of the Bureau of Land Management territories has just begun. Could it be that the successes and battles described in this book would encourage you to greater accomplishments? But take heed: it is lonely work in the wilderness! May you develop the heart and eyes for it. Those of you inclined to look and not act, it is suggested that you visit the de facto wilderness areas not yet enacted.

The 1980 enactment of the 12 areas, added to our exisiting National Wildernesses, came to 19 separate Wildernesses in New Mexico. Five of the areas were additions to previously enacted Wildernesses. The total acreage in 1980 came to 1,468,946 acres of National Wilderness in New Mexico. This is 1.9% of the area of our state. There is no percentage goal but we should not rest until all of the qualified lands are given the protection provided by the Wilderness Act.

The public endeavors and the Congressional actions described above resulted from the realization that wilderness was being swallowed up by land developers of all kinds. These efforts grew out of the earlier activities that led to the selection of the New Mexico areas that were included in the 1978 Endangered American Wilderness Act. The Park Service enactments in that same era derived from the same development threats. So the dilemmas that these 1978 enactments were made to eliminate, created new dilemmas generated by the force of law on both the managers and users. Wilderness lovers considered the trade-off more than worth it.

CHAPTER 8
The Endangered American Wilderness Act and Park Service Enactments of 1978

C ongress apparently thought that there was a sufficient threat pattern to a number of potential wildernesses that they put together a combination wilderness bill which they named The Endangered American Wilderness Act. That legislation was intended to alleviate the various dilemmas associated with each area included. It worked quite well in the short term but it lacked something in later events. In the interim, it became apparent to some members of the general population that there had to be a civilian component to the management of those wildernesses. These areas added such an unfamiliar load to Forest Service Districts and Park Service managers that wilderness lovers saw many events were going uncontrolled.

These wilderness nuts as they were called among themselves realized that it was not enough to obtain a wilderness enactment, but that they had to continue to communicate with the district rangers and even volunteer to do some tasks that there were not enough Agency personnel to do. In some cases, the problems generated more quickly than the Agency people could be trained to take care of them. There were a few fumbles by the well meaning volunteers, also. Admittedly, this is a too brief and perhaps inadequate stage setting for the legislation, but here is what happened a couple of years before the Endangered American Wilderness Act was passed.

In mid-1976 questions started to quietly feed back from the House Interior and Insular Affairs Committee about our New Mexico Omnibus bill. The probings were put gently to try to determine which of our areas were the most threatened by disqualifying activities or trends. We indicated the areas in our Omnibus bill and generated a synopsis of threats of which we were aware and rated the inroads as to which were the most threatening. We submitted our responses through our Senators and Representatives and told the House Committee we were doing it. Despite some filtering of our information, the House Committee staffers did get the primary message during the fall recess of Congress.

The Forest Service had rejected the Sandia Mountain Wilderness proposal during the 1972-73 RARE review on the basis of the claim that the "sights and sounds" of the city of Albuquerque disqualified the adjacent mountain area. Some of the House and Senate Committee members came to Albuquerque quietly and we escorted them into the area of the purported sights and sounds. A couple of them were left breathless when we reached the top of a ridge low on the westside escarpment and showed them the lights of town. They said that every wilderness should have such a delightful contrast. The result was that the Committee on Interior and Insular Affairs submitted House Bill No. 95-540: "Designating Certain Endangered Public Lands for Preservation as Wilderness, Providing for the Study of Additional Endangered Public Land for Such Designation, Furthering the Purposes of the Wilderness Act of 1964, and for Other Purposes."

The bill included both the Sandia and Manzano Mountain Wildernesses (20 miles southeast of Albuquerque) among several others in western states. We were disappointed to see the omission of our Chama River Canyon Wilderness. At that time in 1977, we had a Wilderness Study Commission in the state government (no direct connection with our NMWSC). Our representative and chief honcho for the Chama Area, Jay Sorenson, being on that Commission, managed to bring the fact of the omission to the House Interior Committee staff through our state government communication channels. The consequence was that the Senate version (Report No. 95-490) submitted by Senator Church, corrected the error and also issued a statement, in a subsequent amendment pertaining to the "sights and sounds" argument. Although the Manzano Mountain Wilderness had been in the original draft it was somehow left out of an intermediate mark-up draft and we had to react again with hundreds of citizens' letters to get it restored to the text of the bill. By way of restitution, Senator Church noted in the Congressional Record that "the sights and sounds argument had no basis in the law" referring to the Wilderness Act and that it derived from the erroneous purity pattern of the Forest Service Regulations.

The culmination of the stormy process was the passage in the House and Senate and the signature of President Carter on Public Law 95-237 on February 24, 1978 of the Endangered American Wilderness Act of 1978. It did contain our 30,930 acre Sandia and 37,000 acre Manzano Wilderness Areas along with the 50,300 acre Chama River Canyon Wilderness as well as others throughout the west. The Chama River Canyon Wilderness is about 10 miles upstream from Abiquiu in the north central part of the state. The real accomplishment is that we have two National Wildernesses in our state adjacent to a large metropolitan area (Albuquerque and environs) accessible to large numbers of recreationists without extensive highway travel. Another meaningful by-product of the Endangered Wilderness Act is that the Chama River, where it is contained in its canyon wilderness, is far better protected as a wild river than it could be under the Wild River Act.

The Park Service was aware in 1979 of our NMWSC proposal of a 156,000 acre composite of the Carlsbad and Guadalupe Mountains National Park, including the intervening National Forest between the two parks at either end of the massive prehistoric reef. We called it the Unified Guadalupe Escarpment Wilderness since it extended across the New Mexico-Texas border through two agency jurisdictions.

We made a good map showing the reef as it existed over 30 miles from the extreme ends of the two parks and being connected by the roadless area of the National Forest. The 1974 deadline in the Wilderness Act was quickly approaching. The Forest Service was not ready to consider their portion of the enactment despite the deadline, but the Park Service did introduce, at our request, a bill S.602 on January 29, 1973 to make the roadless portions of each National Park enacted National Wilderness. They thus complied with the intent of the Wilderness Act. However, it was not until October, 1978 that the enactment actually took place. The areas were 46,840 acres in Guadalupe Mountains National Park and 33,125 acres in Carlsbad Caverns National Park, each of these being smaller than the NMWSC had proposed. It is like a poker game in which you bet for bigger stakes but really expect to settle for something less.

We would have preferred to have enactment of the entire reef as wilderness, but we had to await the Forest Service process. The question of an underground wilderness, associated with surface National Wilderness classification, is brought into view. Our claim is that the caves must be considered wild caves with no manmade developments. However, vandalism requires metal gratings or doors over the cave mouths, and some man-made closures of particularly delicate zones within the caves. Consequently, the issue of how wild or natural a discovered cave can be is not treated in the law. Park and agency regulations, if enforceable, can be useful.

Park master plans must be watched carefully, as must Forest Land and Resource Management Plans. Once approved, after having been exposed to public review, they tend to assume something of the force of law. Consequently, wilderness management after enactment must be watched by the public users (owners) to see if the professional servants are neither negligent nor over-zealous. Too much wilderness management can be counterproductive.

CHAPTER 9
The Wilderness Water Dilemma

Drinkable water is becoming a scarce commodity in many parts of the world, including North America. There is a thriving trade in bottled water, as you well know. Each of us must consume at least a quart of water per day in foods or liquid form or we wither and die. Some people get dehydrated unless they have more than that. And then there some, including the Australian bushman, who have learned to get along on less than that, but they are exceptions.

You have heard the litany of water problems many times in different guises. Hospital and hotel water systems have become polluted and have sickened many people. City water systems require continuous taxpayer support or they become antiquated and even dangerous. Ancient Roman settlements had lead pipes conducting water from their aqueducts and other water sources. Some historians think that they have detected lead poisoning symptoms even in the early Roman populace. Wines containing lead compounds were also suspected. Several of today's vintages have been withdrawn from sale for the same suspected reason. The difference today is that we have a test for lead and other contaminants, if we will only use it.

The whole of North America is rich in its foundation of aquifers containing ground water. The Ogallala Aquifer is a dramatic case. The town of Artesia, New Mexico was named for its location near the artesian wells that spouted fresh water above the surface. I saw one well in the early 1940s that still gushed up about a foot or so above the ground level. Continuous pumping of Ogallala water over several state areas has lowered the water level to alarming depths. This is a national problem because the Ogallala Aquifer extends southward from Nebraska to Texas and is several hundred miles wide. There are now thoughts of trying to divert some of the Mississippi River water into the depleted areas. The users of the Mississippi's water suspect that our water engineering may not be good enough to use just the right amount or even decide what that is.

There are many examples of heavily pumped ground waters being replaced by invading brackish and/or salt water. These sources are still being used at a considerable expense of reclaiming processes. Others, instead of paying the bill now, are using increasingly brackish water for agricultural needs, knowing that the land will become less productive the saltier it becomes. Liquid wastes are quietly being injected into old wells and boreholes. Landfill wastes are leaching into water supplies according to EPA and others. Love Canal is only one location that went out of control. We are busy carrying large volumes of solid and liquid wastes to sea. Jacques Cousteau and other pioneers of the undersea domain have sounded the alarm. Our ability to foul our nests seems to be outgrowing our capability of controlling our offal. These are some of the by-products of our civilization. Must we all drink bottled water to survive?

Recharge of the aquifers is a natural process that takes a long time. It depends upon many factors. Rain and other precipitation on the earth's surface is the main input. Industrial processes that generate the components of acid rain are another influence. Conversion of rural farmland to urban dwellings and occupancy changes the surface absorbency of those areas. Plowing land may increase the aquifer recharge rate but it may also lead to soil loss downstream.

The cumulative areas of cities with their millions of acres of parking lots, paved roads, roofs, shopping centers, all reduce the total area that can absorb rainfall. Floods happen when the watershed cannot soak up the precipitation fast enough. Surface water channels and flood plains are often tampered with in a civilized manner. We build "Industrial Parks" in flood plains only to discover that there is something called a twenty-five year flood, or even a fifty year flood. It is hard to tell which one it is when the lights go out. We bulldoze housing sites over dry arroyos, pat the earth down, and build houses thereupon. Some folks have been awakened in the night to hear water gushing in the basement in that old streambed everyone had forgotten.

Our mountain states contain much of our high country in the upland watersheds. Therein lies the dilemma. Many of our wildernesses are in the various watersheds on both sides of the Continental Divide. They are busy absorbing precipitation to recharge some of the aquifers underlying them. Their undisturbed surfaces are nearly optimum sponges for the precipitation that falls on them. Some of the water is transpired by the trees and may become clouds downwind of the mountain crests to rain on the plains.

Many of the de facto wilderness areas on the plains are under Bureau of Land Management jurisdiction. These areas tend to absorb rainfall also, particularly if they are not overgrazed. There is an ongoing series of projects of the U.S. Army Engineers to attempt to slow down the siltation of rivers by tributary streams. Consequently a considerable number of dams are proposed across many intermittent streams that carry large silt loads during annual flooding. The dams should work quite well during their early lives, but they must soon fill up and thereafter be useless or perhaps merely delaying factors when later floods fissure their contents downstream. Such phareatophytes as the salt cedar can get a start in some of these dam silts and may bind the loose deposits well enough to reduce blowing and wind erosion. Public pressures to permit two, three, and four wheeled off-road vehicle rallies on these dry watersheds annually are brought to bear on the BLM land managers. Studies are ongoing to attempt to determine the short and long term effects of such civilized ground disturbances. Who knows that it might prove that the concentrated earth disturbances might assist regeneration of range cover plants. There are similar claims made by the Savory Methods wherein cattle concentrated on limited pastures churn up the range cover rejuvenation processes.

Wilderness watersheds may be optimum from many viewpoints including precipitation absorption. The sparkling water looks good enough to drink, and that is one of the dimensions of the dilemma. The widescale spread of Giardia parasites and the leptospirosis spirochetes endemic in our rural populations (man and beast) makes that water ever suspect as drinking water. Thus far it does appear that such waters passing through gravel and sand aquifers removes most of the infectious elements. When the filter gets overloaded is a moot question. It is hard to be certain unless very recent specific tests of the potable water have been made. Public campground water systems have been shut down because of such uncertainties much to the dislike and dismay of the camping public.

A federal judge ruled on November 25, 1985 that National Wilderness Areas, at least in Colorado, have the water rights to the water therein. The judge instructed the Forest Service to prepare a plan for protecting wilderness water and submit it to him by April 1 1986. (Associated Press Release, Grand Junction, Colorado, dated November 28, 1985.) Water rights in Colorado have been sequestered in every way imaginable since the white man settled in the state. The above Wilderness water decision does not make an ultimate solution any easier.

It raises a whole new set of questions. When the water flows out of the wilderness onto private land, does it suddenly change ownership? If the Wilderness does not cover the entire watershed, does a part of the water belong to the government and if so, how much?

Do in-holdings which were long ago sitting on springs and other active water sources before Wilderness enactment now belong to the government? Will mining and other discharges upstream from wilderness be affected? These and many other elements of the Wilderness water dilemma may be worked out by civilized man's decisions, or will they? Perhaps the wilderness will have a way of its own to reduce the dilemma.

The *High Country News* of December 9, 1985 reported that the ruling could have long term delaying effects upon outstanding Wilderness legislation. The Sierra Club which brought the suit to court indicated that all such matters should get settled before enactment to reduce the possibilities of later contest. They might be saying the same thing.

One of the problems that such a ruling raises is the situation in which a grazing permittee has installed a plastic water line between a spring or water source in a Wilderness and a cattle tank outside the boundary. In several such cases, the permittee has the approval of the District Forest Ranger and many have had such a system in place at the date of enactment of the area. He may have agreed to provide a wildlife watering trough at the source. The question now might be: Should the rancher be charged for the water? If the system did not exist, the rancher might have to haul water in from another souce at some continuing expense. Possibly there is a precedent, but I know of none. The Wilderness Act does allow water reservoirs and the like but does not mention anything about water rights or the sale of water. This is just another small dimension of the wilderness management dilemma.

One issue of considerable importance, as yet unresolved, is the problem of a proposed Hooker Dam. A brief synopsis of the Central Arizona Project (CAP) is necessary for the understanding of the Hooker Dam controversy.

The CAP was originated at mid-century to attempt to forestall the citizens of Arizona from running out of water in the near future, like the year 2000 A.D. The central, most populated part of Arizona had been using water for agriculture and other purposes for more than half a century when some accelerated changes in the water uses became apparent. Citrus orchards, cotton crops, and variants of truck farms were prolific producers.

The city fathers in Phoenix and some of its satellite towns saw the necessity of constructing canals to help distribute the water for such agricultural needs. The canals were built and more orchards proliferated. So did the lawns and trees. The citizens who had come to Arizona for its dry climate began to wonder what was happening to it. The water table started to drop. The hydrologists had earlier discovered an extensive canal system which had been built and used by earlier inhabitants of the Salt River Valley, the prehistoric Indians.

Swamp coolers, otherwise known as evaporative coolers, no longer worked satisfactorily in the built-up areas of the cities. The humidity had become too high. Many people lived in Phoenix during the delightful winters and moved out during the summer months. Then it soon became possible to use refrigerative air conditioning to again make summer living affordable and comfortable. People kept moving in and more of them stayed.

Real estate for homes became more valuable than citrus orchards. Whole retirement villages sprung up with lawns and palm trees. Shopping centers, parking lots, and streets were paved and roofed over to seal the earth from absorption of rain and flood waters. The flooding became more severe. Cities pumped more water for domestic use.

Agriculture moved into open spaces in an outward migration. More dams like Orme and Roosevelt Dams were built. More water was pumped. More salt and brackish water was intruding into the aquifers. The only solution to the problem appeared to be to import water into the area from elsewhere.

Immediately it was concluded that along with damming some of the nearby streams that flooded, that more dams on the Colorado River were needed. Those dams on the Colorado were needed to furnish electrical power to run the pumps to push more water into the Central Arizona populated area. Large aqueducts were soon on the drawing boards. It was also discovered that we were already not delivering the promised amount of water to Mexico out of the Colorado River near Yuma and what we were discharging was salty and much used. It contained various residues from its prior uses. Consequently, a desalting plant was built at Yuma. It helped the discharge quality somewhat.

There were other rivers involved in the Central Arizona Project. The San Carlos River, the Blue River, the San Francisco River, and the Gila River joined in Graham County in eastern Arizona against the New Mexico border. The Gila River with its tributaries, Mangas Creek and Turkey Creek, flooded with great vigor to sometimes join its downstream counterparts in rampaging down the Salt River toward Phoenix and Tempe. So the conclusion was to dam the Gila and the other wild rivers so that Goldwater's basement would not be flooded and a better regulated water supply would be available for Central Arizona. There are other river sources also involved.

The part that involves New Mexico is the proposed damming of the Gila River. There are at least two damsites in contention and a third an adjunct to one of the initial two. Hooker is a damsite located upstream on the Gila River not far below the National Wilderness Boundary in New Mexico. Conner is an alternative damsite well downstream from Hooker. Mangas Creek damsite is upstream from Conner and downstream from Hooker.

An Upper Gila Water Supply Study has recently been rejuvenated in an attempt to reach a conclusion. The Bureau of Reclamation and the Corps of Engineers have entered in an agreement to open the study once more. President Carter had put the Hooker damsite and project to rest. A new administration is thus reopening the "study." The Assistant Interior Secretary, Garrey Carruthers, has said that the "Hooker Dam Association" has requested that the feasibility estimate completion be expedited from the spring of 1986 to the fall of 1984. A Stage I analysis, announced in October 1982, sounds like there is already a firm conclusion that the Hooker Site is the best solution.

The NMWSC does not like the Hooker Dam Site because it would back water up into the Gila National Wilderness Area. It would flood and otherwise destroy the riverine community of fauna and flora of that portion of the Gila Wilderness. It would flood and otherwise destroy archeological artifacts and prehistoric living sites along the river in the affected region. The dam would lose a great deal of water in an evaporation mode due to the high summertime temperatures and low humidity in that desert environment. The water entrapped by such a dam should not benefit the citizens and taxpayers of New Mexico to any major degree. The NMWSC understands that the downstream water rights have been bought up or otherwise obtained by a mining company (presumably by Phelps Dodge). If so, very few private owners downstream will benefit if they no longer live there. The proposed conveyance pipelines from the three dam sites converge at a proposed juncture point west of Silver City.

The Bureau of Reclamation's "Information Packet" stated the following in February 1982: (Stage I Conclusions) "Conner (site) stands out as the preferred plan." However, in October, 1982, the Bureau of Reclamation changed its signals thusly:

Residents of the Cliff-Gila area, members of the Hooker Dam Association, and the New Mexico Interstate Stream Commission felt that the Hooker alternative should not be eliminated because of its flood control potential in the Cliff-Gila area, its greater net yield, and its financial advantages for New Mexcio water users. Therefore, as a direct result of the public comments, the bureau reconsidered its tentative recommendation. Since public acceptability is critical to its planning studies, the Bureau decided to include Hooker Dam and Reservoir in the Stage II studies.

The April 1983, Issue IV, of Bu Rec's "Upper Gila Water Supply Study" newsletter stated that as a result of their December 1982 meeting with the New Mexico Interstate Stream Commission, the Hooker Dam Site was eliminated, and that the Conner Site would be further studied. No reasons were given. Perhaps our miscellaneous letters to Bu Rec and the Stream Commission had some small contribution to the conclusion.

One can see that it could be a full time activity to attempt to protect our enacted National Wildernesses against the seemingly endless threats. New Mexican conservationists have used the legal, legislative route as described in this book.

Other states have had similar experiences. Perhaps accounts of their tribulations are even now being written.

CHAPTER 10
Federal Land Policy and Management Act of 1976 (FLPMA)

The Bureau of Land Management, under The Department of the Interior, had been the custodian of the major part of the nation's public range lands since about 1934. The General Land Office and a successor agency called the Grazing Service preceded the Bureau of Land Management. "The Taylor Grazing Act of 1934 provided those organizations the authority to manage some 140 million acres of depleted grasslands. These were lands that nobody wanted to buy or care for, but everybody wanted to use as long as grass grew on them. The Taylor Grazing Act is probably the first act which the Congress openly acknowledged that portions of the country did not submit well to settlement or unsupervised use. The passage of the Taylor Grazing Act should be celebrated as the day when enormous chunks of the public domain would no longer be turned over to private enterprise; not for a price, and certainly not for free." (*Wilderness*, Fall 1982, Zaslowsky).

The BLM operated without an organic act until the passage of the Federal Land Policy and Management Act of October 21, 1976. It actually managed quite well within the confines of and through the use of a number of selected laws pertinent to public land management. It was FLPMA that mandated the wilderness activities. Under Section 603 of FLPMA, the BLM is directed to make a wilderness study of its lands within fifteen years of the 1976 enactment. The Wilderness Act is to provide the criteria for selection, and the lands selected for study are to be managed in the interim in such a manner as not to impair the suitability of those areas for preservation as Wilderness, "subject, however, to the continuation of existing mining and grazing uses and mineral leasing" (on the date of the Act).

Section 603 requires the Secretary of the Interior to have mineral surveys made by the Geological Survey and the Bureau of Mines on the areas considered suitable for Wilderness. It also specifies a report to the President of the Secretary's recommendations. The President is to then advise the President of the Senate and the Speaker of the House, and include a map and boundary definition, all within two years from the receipt of the Secretary's recommendation. The Congress may or may not act upon the recommendations. The area will be managed as Wilderness until an Act of Congress is passed or rejected.

FLPMA contains a change in the reporting of mining claims. In the past under the 1882 General Mining Law it was only necessary to report or make a mining claim recording with the County Clerk and Recorder in the county in which the mining was done or proposed. Under FLPMA Section 314 it is now required that the owner of an unpatented lode on placer mining claim file a record annually of location and a notice of intention to retain the claim (and do the annual assessment work) at an office of the BLM appropriate to the location of the claim. Failure to file will be considered to be abandonment of the claim.

Mining claims on National Forest Lands are recorded in the nearest BLM Office, but the operation plan must first be approved by the Forest Supervisor upon the recommendation of the District Ranger. County registration is still required by state law.

One of the requirements of FLPMA is that the BLM (or Secretary of the Interior) is to manage and maintain the public lands as a renewable resource. One example is that some overgrazed lands can be withdrawn from permitted grazing as one means of accomplishing recovery or renewal of the land's capacity to accommodate further or future grazing.

A specific example, but not one relating to a Wilderness Study Area (WSA), is laughable if it were not so tragic in its consequences. Some of the satellite photos of the southwest showed the demarcation of the U.S./ Mexican border in a strange way. All of the lands north of the border were overgrazed to the point of their being markedly more barren than those immediately south of the border. The BLM, stung at this realization of overgrazing and knowing that much of the land photographed was theirs, decided to do something about the overgrazing situation. They had to start somewhere. One of the areas chosen to be rested and given some other restoration was the Rio Puerco, west of Albuquerque. One or more of the grazing permittees took the case to court and was turned down.

The matter seemed to be settled. But wait. A James G. Watt of Denver, representing an organization called The Mountain States Legal Foundation, appealed the case to a higher court and won. The BLM was aghast. That was before the 1980 election. Imagine their chagrin when they discovered that the new Reagan administration appointed the same Watt to be Secretary of Interior, their new boss!

Although it was surely not unique to our state, the Sagebrush Rebellion was fueled in part by such withdrawals of grazing permits for rest and restoration of the public lands. Some of the affected ranchers who had substantial grazing permits on public lands joined the "Rebellion" to attempt to have such public lands transferred to the states from the federal government. They had been able to more easily monopolize grazing permit lands owned by the states. The state is required by law (in New Mexico) to manage its lands for the highest economic return. This often has been the reason for selling many tracts to the highest bidder.

It has been a continuing battle in New Mexico for the recreationists to obtain access to hunting and fishing areas across or through state permitted lands. Cutting of fences, smashing of gates, and leaving of trash by a messy public has caused understandable bitterness on the part of the ranchers.

The same FLPMA (Act) fueled more anti-wilderness sentiment because it urged a BLM wilderness inventory process more rapidly than the public land users could understand its ramifications. The wide, open BLM spaces were not easily travelled on foot or horseback. The permittees in some instances were driven to using motorcycles of several varieties for tending their stock instead of only horsemen. They knew that FLPMA Wilderness enactment would eliminate motorized access. They also feared that more people would be attracted by the label of Wilderness, and that their virtual possession of the public land would be threatened.

Some of the smaller ranchers and permittees did not join the "Rebellion" because they could foresee that the bigger and more wealthy interests could buy the lands transferred to the states. That could put the small rancher with his smaller BLM or Forest Service Grazing Permit area out of business. Meanwhile the new administration read the Sagebrush Rebellion "as a mandate to transfer public lands to state and private ownership." Now the Watt shoe was on the other foot. He was heard to make one of his famous, off-the-cuff "one-liners" to the effect that the Sagebrush Rebellion was dead (or over). To the contrary, however, the Reagan administration has notified all of the Federal Agencies to inventory all of their lands for the determination of lands surplus to their needs and to initiate steps to dispose of them.

The administration of public lands by the states has been marred by the difficulty of some of the states to hire the best-trained professionals. Such jobs are subject to political wind changes to some degree whereas the civil service system of the federal government has been more stable for land managers.

The surplus land disposal thrust has stirred both the agency personnel and the public. Under the Title II of FLPMA, Sections 201 through 203, both Secretaries of Interior and Agriculture are instructed to do a comprehensive land use plan which provides for both land acquisition and disposition. For example, on November 25, 1982 the Secretary of Agriculture John Block said that his department had begun reviewing 140 million acres of national forest lands to determine whether some parcels should be sold. This was supposedly to alleviate our national debt. Those people and companies capable of buying the public lands will benefit at the expense of those pa..s of the public now using those parcels who are unable to buy them. New Mexico could become privately owned, like Texas where hunters have to pay land owners for hunting privileges.

Secretary Block is quoted (UPI) as saying that the Forest Service has identified 51 million acres out of the 191 million acres nationwide which will not be sold. If that ration of land for sale applies (51/191 = 26.7%) to the other federal land agencies, our nation will own only 8.6% of its land. At present, one-third of our land is owned by all of its citizens nationwide. New Mexico, only by coincidence, is also one-third public land. The people in the outdoor organizations in New Mexico are beginning to become concerned as are similar groups throughout the nation. We are not yet ready to trade our freedom for a mess of potage.

The checkerboard ownership of the lands has already caused much interference with the rational management of the public common. We could not afford to build railroads at our own hourly labor rates so we imported laborers from China and Ireland. Our government induced large capital investors to build the railroads by giving them odd-numbered sections along their right-of-way. It is somewhat amusing that our nation settled the vanquished Indians on reservations occupying supposedly worthless lands only to later discover that those lands were rich in oil, gas, and coal deposits. In New Mexico, not only do the Indians make their own decisions on reservation resource development, but they contest development on Indian occupied public lands adjacent to their reservations. When the oil companies and power utilities try to buy some of the checkerboard land over oil, gas, and coal deposits from the BLM, the Santa Fe Railroad, and the State of New Mexico, it is likely to be contested by the Indians as land traditionally lived upon by Indians. This has proven to be a delaying tactic but generally an unsuccessful one.

Uranium has also been discovered and mined on these Indian lands as well as on the checkerboarded ownership areas. To complicate matters further, some of the lands have reverted to government ownership for failure to pay taxes. In some instances the BLM has acquired old Spanish Land Grants without getting the mineral rights in the deal. Other situations have arisen such as the Department of Interior and Wildlife Service's purchase of state lands on the Salt Creek National Wilderness near Roswell, New Mexico. The state withheld the mineral rights and subsequently issued a drilling lease to a Yates Petroleum Corporation. Several of the BLM Wilderness Study Areas are similarly complicated by the same "split estate" ownership schism. The Yates/Salt Creek case is covered in Chapter 12.

The BLM was already well into the FLPMA directed wilderness study process before the drastic changes induced by the new administration. They had their hands full trying to cope with the cloudy ownership problems described in the preceding two paragraphs. The signals from their new bosses came down their line organization in various and sometimes conflicting forms. One strong message arrived at the field level in the form of reduced budgets for some items. The district managers tried to interpret some of their Interior Secretary's one-liner pronouncements which he made during some of his after-dinner utterances. Confusion could occasionally be detected by the public when the BLM line would act on some of the new signals.

The conservation organizations and the New Mexico Wilderness Study Committee had been working along with the BLM on the FLPMA directed wilderness studies in the public involvement phases. Enthusiasm for the legal process began to wain both in the Agency and the citizen sectors. Several people expressed their qualms to the effect that the mountains of work would come to nothing when the final lists were subjected to Secretary Watt's approval. Even as a November 24, 1982 deadline for completion of a list of BLM wilderness study areas for public review was met by the BLM districts in the state, articles appeared in the *Albuquerque Journal* about the uncertainty of Washington level endorsement.

On December 30, 1982, the Secretary of the Interior published in the *Federal Register* (Vol. AT No. 251) a notice amending previous

71

wilderness inventory decisions in accordance with three Interior Board of Land Appeals (IBLA) decisions. These decisions involved areas smaller than 5000 acres, lands where the federal government owns the surface but not the mineral rights (split estate) and areas contiguous to designated wilderness. This dictum eliminated twelve WSAs in New Mexico. We have not become reconciled to this turn of events. The New Mexico Wilderness Study committee may include some of the eliminated areas in an omnibus bill of our own. The IBLA decisions nationwide do not fit our state circumstances very equably.

Seven of the WSAs were restudied after the split-estate areas were removed. A Supplemental Draft Environmental Assessment was issued by BLM in August, 1983 with four of the areas being recommended as suitable for Wilderness. They were the 8,780 acre Ignacio Chavez, the 23,857 acre Aden Lava Flow, the 41,293 acre Big Hatchet Mountains, and the 147,100 acre West Potrillo Mountains/Mount Riley. Eagle Peak, Mesita Blanca, and Alamo Hueco Mountains were not recommended in the Assessment. From a detached viewpoint, one could assure that four out of seven is better than none, but who is detached? BLM is awaiting the public reaction to make the final adjustments. If the state land inholdings and mineral rights could be incorporated, the enacted Wilderness Areas could be easier to manage and administer.

CHAPTER 11
The Elena Gallegos Land Grant Acquisition, a Landmark Wilderness Case

The west side or escarpment of the Sandia Mountains is deeply pierced by three large canyons immediately adjacent to one another. From a distance, perhaps as far away as the Rio Grande, they look like one big canyon dividing the mountain into two parts. These canyons are Domingo Baca, Pino, and Bear Canyons. They are wooded, have some running water, and are excellent grazing lands. Also, having no roads in the upper parts, they are wilderness. However, they are and have been privately owned for centuries. Therein lies the story.

The Endangered American Wilderness Act of 1978 (see Chapter 6) enacted the 30,930 acre Sandia Mountain Wilderness as one of its actions. You recall that the Sandia Mountain is the abrupt highland immediately east of Albuquerque. The Cibola National Forest Boundary and the east Albuquerque city limits generally coincide in the Sandia foothills. The Sandia Mountain National Wilderness boundary also almost coincides with the Forest boundary along the mountain front.

The three canyons previously mentioned were contained within an Elena Gallegos Grant which ran in a rectangular strip from the Rio Grande on the west to the crest of the Sandia Mountain on the east. The north and south boundaries, although not quite parallel, are about four miles apart. The original grant was approximately 35,000 acres. The Spanish Land Grant was conveyed to a Diego Montoya by then Governor Diego de Vargas in 1694. The title passed to Elena Gallegos sometime between 1716 and 1731. It subsequently passed along the line to her heirs. Through the years various of the western parts had been sold and in about 1931, Albert Simms, Sr. acquired what remained of the grant. A Simms legacy endowed an Academy Trust as custodians of the Albuquerque Academy. Consequently, throughout the 1970s and early 1980s, the Academy Trust had custody and administration of the grant.

The wilderness or upper part of the grant is a three by three mile bite out of the Sandia Mountain Wilderness and contains the three aforementioned large canyons climbing up the west face of the mountain. The macroclimate of that upper part of the grant is such that it has more precipitation than the surrounding areas. Its more moderate climate and flora attract deer and other wildlife particularly as a winter range.

Many of us in the New Mexico Wilderness Study Committee had been acquainted with this grant area of the mountain through permit or approval of its caretakers in our various interests of hiking, mountain climbing, bird and wildlife watching, and bow hunting in season. Consequently, in the early 1970s we anticipated that a future Sandia Mountain Wilderness would be incomplete without the portion in the grant. The NMWSC mentioned this opinion to Senator Montoya during a general briefing. He appeared to agree.

A tramway to an upper ski area terminal and restaurant on the crest of the mountain was built in the mix-sixties. The lower terminal was built just immediately to the north of the grant northern boundary. The tram cars and cables cross over the Domingo Baca Canyon outside of the grant since the canyon trends northeast. There is a non-wilderness corridor underneath the tram route up the side of the mountain. Only one house existed in the grant in the 1970s. It was in Bear Canyon just below the waterfall. The house was burned down by vandals in the early seventies. It has since been rebuilt.

Shortly after the tram was built, a housing development known as Sandia Heights occupied the land adjacent to the lower tram terminal due west of Domingo Baca Canyon outside the grant. The houses are not tract houses. Most have been nicely worked into their immediate environment and command a wonderful view of both the mountain and the city.

Some cattle have been grazed on the grant for many years, but it is far from overgrazed. Otherwise it has been unused. A couple of airplane crashes and a few inadvertent balloon landings have done little permanent damage.

In about 1975, it became known that the remainder of the grant might be up for sale. The McDonnell-Douglas Aircraft Company of St. Louis attempted to make an offer to the government in which it would purchase the grant in return for title to the government plant it occupies in St. Louis, and thereby turn the grant title over to the federal government. The newspapers had it the other way around. Anyway, the deal hung fire for a long time and then fell through.

The City (of Albuquerque) Open Spaces Task Force had been actively attempting to solve most of the problems, particularly on the perimeter of the city as they related to parks, recreation, and other open space needs of the citizens. One of their concerns dealt with the difficulties of furnishing city services (water, sewage, gas, garbage collection, and fire protection) to areas having steep road access, generally above a ten percent grade. There is now a City Council resolution addressing that principle. It passed in January, 1978.

When it became evident that the McDonnell-Douglas Aircraft proposal was not going to fly towards the fall of 1976, the N.M. Wilderness Study Committee pointed out to our Senators and Representatives that the Land and Water Conservation Fund normally provided funds for the acquisition of inholdings in National Wildernesses. It appeared a bit premature to consider the Sandias as National Wilderness (RARE II was not yet completed) but we pointed out that a change in National Forest Boundaries had to be the first step in acquisition of additional National Forest in any event. Consequently, Senator Domenici presented a bill (S.553) on February 1, 1977 to change the forest boundary to cut across the grant above a line that approximates the ten percent slope line.

A year of jockeying went on. The county (Bernalillo) became involved and the state made a study and some recommendations, including the promise of a million dollars to aid in some future transaction. A value for the purchase of the grant lands was bandied about.

The Albuquerque Journal carried a story in 1977 that Mayor Kinney was undecided about making the Sandia Mountain a National Wilderness although he favors keeping the mountain "as untouched as possible." The same article indicated that his wife, Carol, said that the wilderness designation would be a "trememdous advantage" to the Albuquerque metropolitan area — "to serve our local people well." Subsequently, the Sandia Mountain National Wilderness was enacted on February 24, 1978 (see Chapter 8).

The Forest Service watched the ebb and flow of the matters pertaining to the grant, and attempted to determine if the Trust would be interested in land trades. Since the grant extends all the way to the crest of the mountain, the acquisition of at least the upper reaches appeared to be a reasonable goal. To foreshorten this tale, Public Law 95-614 was introduced and passed into law on November 8, 1978, providing for changing the National Forest Boundary to include those upper reaches of the grant within the National Forest, and including $12 million for its purchase. It also stipulated that 640 acres of the lower reaches were to be purchased by the city for such open spaces purposes as it required. The Sandia Heights development company had made an offer on that lower parcel. It is interesting to note that the price for that lower parcel approaches that for the upper portion, even though it is only about eight percent of the larger area. The part of the grant in negotiation totalled about 8000 acres.

The bill to change the National Forest Boundary originally had the words "intended wilderness" in the drafts. Senator Jackson (D.-Wash.) pointed out that there was no such legal land classification and deleted these words from the final bill. Our delegation (Senator Domenici and Representative Lujan) had told us that they "will introduce wilderness enactment as soon as the federal government obtains title to the land."

The Public Law (95-614) provided the basis for the Forest Service to proceed with a purchase of the grant lands in concert with the Albuquerque acquisition of a section of it for open space purposes. The Land and Water Conservation Fund (LWC) had some $285 million in it slated for fiscal year 1981; and $20 million of that amount identified for the Forest Service purchase of the grant. Albuquerque's council had prepared its equal value negotiations to be able to commit about $5 million to the Academy Trust. Albuquerque's Mayor David Rusk, with the aid of Newly Reinhart, Tim Kraft, and John O'Donnell (our city lobbyist in Washington), managed much of the process. Virginia Sears, our state aide in Washington, D.C., also added the Governor's force to the equation.

The Carter administration submitted a balanced budget for FY 81 but when the Congress had finished juggling it, it was some $38 billion overspent. The LWC Fund had been cut to about $140 million, and the grant line item was deleted. Senator Jackson and other powerful legislators assured their own priority projects in their own states. Normally, the LWC Fund has not been an instrument for budget balancing. Meanwhile, there were some new members on the Academy Trust Board and they were having second thoughts at the $25 million and were even toying with commercial development proposals attributed to some real estate promoters.

Mayor David Rusk was steadfast in his commitment to live up to Albuquerque's part of the deal and transferred ownership of a large, revenue producing, underground garage in the Civic Center to the Academy Trust as "honest money." He was ridiculed for the action partially because of subsequent events dragging out without closure of the sale. He had his council's endorsement, the county and state's support, and the Carter administration's assurance in back of him. He also had a lot of courage in the face of budget problems generated by rapidly rising costs in Albuquerque and elsewhere. The Albuquerque Open Spaces Task Force also was very consistent in its conclusions pertaining to the necessity of obtaining the grant.

When the new administration blew onto the scene, one of the first actions of the new Interior Secretary was to drastically cut the Land and Water Conservation Fund under his jurisdiction. That stopped the Forest Service negotiations cold. The LWC Fund was to have been the source of the $20 million needed to augment the $5 million to be paid by the city of Albuquerque.

All parties started to rethink what had to be done to progress toward a culmination. The private land developer reopened his communication with the Academy. The Academy, under a new chairman, made several moves of encouragement toward all parties. The Forest Service started to talk about trading equal value lands. the state reaffirmed its $1 million offer. The press castigated Mayor Rusk for having given away the City Parking Lot without compensation.

New appraisals were being solicited by the Forest Service in March, 1980. At that time the purchase price had been set by the Academy Trust at $24.5 million. The bill in Congress had not yet changed the authorization from $12 million to $20 million for the Forest Service's part (7,461 acres). On April 16, 1980, the Congressional Record reported the passage of the increase amendment. This was propelled to some degree by the adept blandishments of our state aide in Washington, D.C. She knew exactly what was going on in the Senate Committee on Energy and Natural Resource's "Business Meeting."

It was on May 29, 1980 that President Reagan signed the bill to purchase the grant. Representative Lujan asked that an unspecified amount in the fiscal year 1981 budget of the LWC Fund be reprogrammed for the initial payment on the purchase. The friction between Secretary Watt and several of the Congressional Committee was beginning to show up. The LWC Fund was his whipping boy, a powerful tool for or against the various states projects he wanted to hold back upon or move.

The bills previously signed and amended had talked about money but there was no appropriation bill to enable the intent of the grant purchase bills. The Bureau of the Budget did not have any wilderness friends in it after the new administration worked over the membership. Consequently, land exchanges began to look like the more fruitful route. It was becoming quite clear during April of 1981 that a deadline of April 1982 might have no solution. Congressman Lujan met several times with the Academy Trustees during the frustrating periods. Senator Schmitt occasionally went with him but tossed the hot potato back to Mayor Rusk to complete the negotiations for the grant purchase. He knew that it would become an election issue in the mayoral race even then heating up.

The city election in 1981 deposed Mayor Rusk and installed former Mayor Harry Kinney. The City Garage had been one of the critical issues. The new mayor was thinking it was a no-win situation. The new city council was doing a meditation to understand the city's commitments and options. The Open Space Task Force was not certain of its continuance early in the second Kinney administration but soon were endorsed by the mayor and the city council. A few of us suspected that Carol Kinney's opinion carried some weight in the matter.

It was during the period of mayoral transition that Rex Funk and Marion Cottrell came up with the idea of the addition of a quarter-cent city sales tax to raise the purchase price in several years. It was determined that the city council had the authority to levy the additional tax without a referendum. Some public meetings were held in which much public support was evident. The newspapers, radio, and TV made much of the idea. The city was to obtain equal value properties from the Forest Service in return for the grant property it was to receive from Albuquerque after the city purchased the grant from the Albuquerque Trust. The added tax was passed by the city council to start July 1, 1982. $25 million was estimated to take about two and one-half years to accrue.

April, 1982 came and went without a purchase being made. The Purchase Agreement was signed on June 30, 1982 at a cost of $24,500,000. The City Garage produced a credit of $1,600,500, reducing the balance to $22,899,500, the base price payment. The city borrowed the money on the strength of the additional sales tax revenue to meet the closing date of July 1, 1982. There were many features associated with the closure of the sale that our conservation community did not like. These had to be negotiated during the delay between the April deadline and the June purchase date. A couple of surprises, for example, were the fact that the mineral rights were reserved to the Academy Trust and also that a Bear Canyon Scenic Easement Area of 270 acres with road right-of-way was withheld from the sale. Remember that burned house that was rebuilt? It is the one near the Bear Canyon waterfall and within the Scenic Easement. Several limitations on the use of the City Park Property (640 acres) were included in the Purchase Agreement. These limitations have little to do with the wilderness aspect of the adjacent National Wilderness so they will not be enumerated. The park is to be named for its donor Albert G. Simms as specified in the agreement. In all, Mayor Kinney did a good job in riding the negotiations to successful conclusions.

The next event reported was in the October 7, 1982 *Albuquerque Tribune*. President Reagan signed into law legislation adding 7,986 acres of National Wilderness to the existing Sandia Mountain National Wilderness. It went on to say that 32,800 acres of New Mexico federal land would be given to the city of Albuquerque in exchange for the Gallegos tract, and then quoted a strange figure of $14.3 million as the purchase price. This figure was not confirmed or derived from the Purchase Agreement. The acreage figures in the bill were also in error. They were pre-survey estimates.

This last action finally accomplished the end result so long striven for by so many people in the Albuquerque area. The addition of the Elena Gallegos Grant wild area of 6,257 acres accomplishes a 37,355 acre Sandia Mountain National Wilderness. The gross acreage is 37,482 within the legal boundary, but the reduction by the 117 acre Calkins inholding in Del Agua Canon brings the figure to the 37,355.

One of the spark plugs that kept the dream alive and pursued was Rex Funk, a long-time member and later chairman of the Open Spaces Task Force. He was subsequently hired by the city to be the caretaker-custodian of the City Park now that the upper grant lands have been transferred to the Forest Service for safekeeping as National Wilderness.

Mary Olin Harrell, a longtime Task Force member, continued with a successful resolve to generate and have installed a permanent monument or memorial to Phil Tollefsrud, a well-known conservationist. Elsewhere in the Sandias, we have tried to have a trail named for him. There are many other people in the Task Force, city councils, Forest Service, and Congress that deserve special mention and thanks for their fair mindedness, community spirit, and actions beyond the call of duty. Victor Marshall and Jay Sorenson were excellent chairmen when times were grim. Fortunately, others are too many to mention individually.

A by-product of the transaction is that the city of Albuquerque is placed in a strange role, that of selling large amounts of real estate. The *Albuquerque Journal* had a feature article on November 26, 1982 by Nancy Harbent, a staff writer. It indicated that 18,600 acres of traded land were being negotiated in parcels throughout the state. The city council hired real estate consultant Jim Achen for one year. Both the Forest Service and the Bureau of Land Management were hard put to add up enough trade lands that were negotiable on short notice. I am aware that there is some discrepancy between the 18,600 figure and that authorized in the October, 1982 legislation naming 32,800 acres. Perhaps all of the trade lands had not been transferred as of November, 1982.

The foregoing has been an attempt to present all of the legislation actions pertaining to the protracted acquisition of the wilderness portion of the Elena Gallegos Grant for addition to the Sandia Mountain National Wilderness. Parts of the story have been left out relating to the other open space considerations for the City Park, the remaining National Forest lands, the easements for roads and reservoirs outside the Wilderness Area. The Academy Trust could do a book of their own presenting all of the considerations that they had to make and resolve. The Forest Service and BLM could publish a tract encompassing all of the turmoil and accomplishment in their part of the negotiations.

One can conclude that the whole process of acquiring part of the grant for wilderness was far from humdrum. It was exasperating, challenging, exhilarating, protracted, and above all, rewarding. It may have been one of the most complicated and difficult wilderness additions attempted to date. Our role as the New Mexico Wilderness Study Committee was one largely of behind the scenes draft bill writing in conjunction with the congressional staff people, long distance telephone calls, letters to editors, public education, and many diverse discussions of alternatives with people of all walks and fields concerned. This book attests to the fact that it was not our only task during the period of its eminence.

A short distance from the northwest corner of the Elena Gallegos Grant boundary is the Sandia Pueblo boundary. A recent rediscovery of the Sandia Pueblo Reservation boundary documentation has been claimed as proof that the eastern boundary of the reservation is roughly along the Sandia Mountain crest. If the Indian ownership is established, it might further deepen the wilderness dilemma since land management under Indian control has been even more variable than that of the U.S. Forest Service. It would put a large part of the Sandia Mountain National Wilderness into Sandia Pueblo control. We know of no National Wilderness which is now under Indian administration.

CHAPTER 12
Mining and Mineral Exploration in New Mexico Wilderness

The Wilderness Act in Section 4 (d) (3) permits mining, prospecting, and oil and gas development under the mining laws and in accordance with regulations to protect wilderness values for nineteen years in Wilderness lands of the national forests. The cut-off date was January 1, 1984. Other controlling legislation subsequently enacted such as the National Environmental Policy Act and the Federal Lands Management and Planning Act tended to stifle much mining and mineral exploration in our New Mexico Wilderness. The NEPA provisions called for an EIS, an Environmental Impact Statement, to be prepared by the land agency involved. The FLPMA legislation specified that leases to do any such mining functions in National Wilderness must be obtained from the BLM.

Until the spring of 1980, there had been only one attempt of any size to prospect or otherwise assess mineral values within any New Mexico Wilderness. A road was bulldozed into the White Mountain Wilderness in the late 1960s to a site which was believed to contain molybdenum. The exploration was considered to be fruitless and the road was blocked and otherwise made impassable to most vehicles.

In September, 1980 three oil and gas leases were issued to two oil and gas development companies to slant drill under the pending Capitan Mountain Wilderness from BLM lands adjacent to and outside of the wilderness. The Capitan Mountain Wilderness was enacted late in December by the Congress and signed by the President. There was no public knowledge at the time of enactment that such leases had been issued. In late January, 1981, Secretary Watt was appointed.

The Wilderness Society discovered some documents pertaining to the agreement some time in September, 1981. Our congressional Representative Manuel Lujan soon had word of the lease issuance and was perturbed that he had not been notified of such drilling leases in his district.

Capitan Mountain is the only east-west trending mountain in New Mexico; all of the others are north-south oriented. A large, hot, molten magma stock pushed a thick limestone bed and other formations upward for at least three thousand feet above its surroundings. Later erosion left the more resistant parts standing about three thousand feet above the surrounding surface. The top of the mountain is about ten thousand feet in altitude.

The Delaware Basin in southeastern New Mexico has produced most of the state's oil and gas discovered to date. The oil and gas companies have made their heaviest finds in the area about fifty miles to the southeast of Capitan Mountain.

Some isolated drillings have produced little more than carbon dioxide and brackish water much closer than fifty miles. The geologists of some of the energy companies theorized that there could be oil or gas showings along the edge or contact zone of the large capitan magma laccolith where it penetrated the bedding plane of the San Andres limestone. They applied for a drilling lease to find out.

In late November, the House Interior and Insular Affairs Committee had voted 40 to 1 to call a six-month moratorium on Wilderness Leasing. Secretary Watt did not feel much bound by the moratorium.

A number of events happened in rapid fire order. On January 29, 1982, Secretary Watt announced that he was agreeing to a one-year moratorium on issuing any new leases nationwide. Conservationists observed that Watt's statement "was a transparent effort to fool the American public into thinking he is in favor of protecting Wilderness Areas when all he is doing is putting the decision past the political season (November elections) this year." On February 15, 1982 the House Committee started to talk again about banning Wilderness mining and drilling. On February 21, 1982 the Secretary (Watt) said that the administration would propose legislation to amend the Wilderness Act to protect the 80 million acres of land until the year 2000. This is known as a Watt field reversal. The National Sierra Club filed suit on February 23, 1982 in Albuquerque to force Secretary Watt to cancel the three oil and gas leases until hearings and an environmental review could be accomplished.

When Watt's NBC "Meet the Press" statement came out in writing, it had a 1984 deadline for any additional National Forest

Wilderness legislation and 1988 for BLM land. Those provisions and the year 2000 ban were in the first draft of a bill that was later introduced by Representative Manuel Lujan. The conservationists started to call the bill "Watt's Anti-Wilderness Bill." Others, less politely said that it was a covert attempt "to gut the Wilderness Act."

Rep. Lujan introduced the H.R. 6542 bill at the administration's request since he was the Majority Leader of the House Interior Committee. He stated that he was doing it with every intention to amend it to achieve a more practical result. He asked for a television meeting with us (the NMWSC) in June, 1982. We made a number of suggestions such as dropping all of the deadlines, including the year 2000, and added the concept of non-destructive testing for oil, gas, and minerals. We pointed out that the Wilderness Act, as is, suited us; and that if the Congress wanted to give Wilderness interim protection against drilling, etc., until the January 1984 mineral activity closure in the Act takes place, to do it simply and directly.

Rep. Lujan must have taken our suggestions seriously because a revised version of the bill came out renamed The Wilderness Protection Act of 1982. It had features that we could live with, and it passed the House in August. The bill passed after two weakening amendments offered by Congressman Don Young (R.-Alaska) were soundly defeated. One would have allowed seismic explosive exploration, and the other would delete protection of Forest Service Wilderness Study areas under consideration since RARE II legislation was enacted. An identical SB-2801 is now in the Senate Committee. Senator Domenici's staff told us that chances for passage are slim if any extended debate is expected, and that the energy companies feel Wilderness leases are "not worth the hassle."

It began to look like the Senator's staff was right in their assessment. The Capitan slant drilling lease was abandoned, and the leases to drill in the Gila were not pursued when it looked too difficult to do an environmental impact statement. There are three of the ten leases on the Aldo Leopold still unresolved. The one on the Manzano Mountain Wilderness is an approved lease for exploratory drilling on the west side just south of Comanche Canyon. John Barnitz, the Mountainair Ranger, told me that he had put a hold on the activity on orders from Washington, D.C. through his line organization. There were some well drillers on an adjoining private property that gave the grazing permittee in the area the impression that they had good enough indications to continue drilling. The same feeling had apparently carried over to the Wilderness leasee who was on hold.

A House Appropriations subcommittee voted on a rider

November 18, 1982 to prohibit Secretary Watt from approving oil and gas leases in Federal Wilderness Areas for another year. It was somewhat strange that this action came from the subcommittee charged with the money bill financing the Department of Interior. Watt's 1982 ban date ran out on December 17, 1982. The subcommittee felt that the full Committee and the House would approve the recommended money bill for the Department and its rider. Such a continuing ban would be applied through September 30, 1983. That would leave three months of vulnerability until the deadline covered by the Wilderness Act took over. However, if the Wilderness Protection Act of 1982 passed, the ban would not have to hang on the money-bill rider. Wilderness support was showing up from many different levels of government.

While awaiting the lame duck session of Congress to consider and act on the Wilderness Protection Act of 1982, the quiet was suddenly disturbed again by a series of actions that seem to be so typically New Mexican in nature. The date was November 1, 1982. Yates Petroleum Corporation started blading a road across some BLM land adjacent to our Salt Creek Wilderness near Roswell in the southeastern part of the state. The road was completed some four days later and drill rigs were arriving at the site within the Wilderness.

This is a prime case of the split estate. The federal government bought the disputed area from the state of New Mexico in 1954. The state retained the mineral rights. In 1972 the state Oil and Gas Division in the Land Office issued a lease having a ten-year period in which exploration was to have taken place or lose the lease. On the last day of the ten-year period, Yates Petroleum dug a symbolic hole with a hand shovel just hours before the lease's midnight expiration. A Department of Interior Attorney in Washington wrote a letter to Yates saying that the department had no legal objection to the drilling. So Yates went ahead with its project.

On November 2, 1982, Bob Burnett, Vice President of the New Mexico Wildlife Federation, was quail hunting in the Bitter Lake National Wildlife Refuge. He found a newly bladed road and a drilling rig in the Salt Creek Wilderness Area. He called the Wildlife Refuge office where the staff was unaware of the activity. He subsequently went to Washington, D.C. to testify before the Public Lands and National Park Subcommittee.

Caught by surprise, U.S. Fish and Wildlife Service cited Yates on Wednesday, November 3, 1982 for trespassing. Yates continued to drill for about an hour and then stopped. The firm asked the Fish and Wildlife Service (Dept. of Interior) for permission to drill through the federally owned surface as early as September, 1982 but had been turned down on the basis of the Interior money-bill rider previously mentioned. U.S. District Judge Juan Burciaga issued a temporary restraining order on Wednesday, November 10, 1982 to halt drilling. Later that day an amended order was issued giving Yates limited access to the site "to maintain the borehole."

Wednesday morning November 3, 1982 a group of environmentalists, led by Dave Foreman, representing "Earth First," barricaded the road at the Wilderness Boundary with tents and flags (American & Don't Tread on Me). Dave is one of our former chairmen of NMWSC. A deputy sheriff threatened to arrest the obstructionists but nothing happened when the judge's restraining order appeared. Congressman John Seiberling called a meeting of the House Subcommittee on Public Lands to determine why the Interior Department had not taken stronger action to stop the drilling. In his opening remarks, Seiberling called the Salt Creek dispute "a test of the will power of the administration to protect wilderness areas in the face of a clear violation of the law" (Albuquerque Journal, November 11, 1982). The case in point was that Yates went onto the federal lands without an access permit despite earlier attempts to obtain one. The Department of Interior denied the foot-dragging charge and cited the no-trespass order on Yates as proof.

A hearing held in Albuquerque on November 18, 1982 by Judge Burciaga issued a permanent injunction blocking Yates from continued drilling in the wilderness area. Attorneys for Yates Petroleum said that they would appeal the ruling to the 10th Circuit Court of Appeals in Denver. Under the terms of the state lease, the drilling could not be shut down for more than twenty days after which the lease would be automatically terminated.

Yates retained the Denver Mountain States Legal Foundation. Being on their board of directors, Yates thought of them, of course. It had nothing to do with the fact that Secretary Watt had been with that organization at the time he was appointed. The appeal was made at the Appeals Court in Denver on November 29, 1982. The court extended Yates' lease and Yates was barred from further drilling until a full hearing could be held in January, 1983. The court order allowed Yates Petroleum to "maintain the hole to prevent cave in." Peyton Yates said that the firm might elect to remove the rig (Albuquerque Journal, November 30, 1982).

The Department of the Interior's Fish and Wildlife Service issued a drilling permit on December 27, 1982 to Yates Petroleum to resume drilling in the disputed area. The company was under court order not to drill in the area until a January hearing in federal court could be held. Secretary Watt was at least keeping the lawyers and congressmen busy. The Department of the Interior was leaning on their interpretation of the Wilderness Act that prior leases for mineral exploration would be honored after enactment. Something was backward here since the Salt Creek Wilderness was enacted in 1970 and the state permit was issued in 1972. If there had been a state drilling permit issued before or prior to the 1970 enactment, there would have been no contest.

Subsequently in early February 1983, the Tenth Circuit Court of Appeals in Denver removed the drillng ban, Yates Petroleum having received a drilling permit from the BLM. On February 7, 1983, the Roswell Assocated Press article "Salt Creek Well Yields Natural Gas" sounded like it was a rather final epitaph. However, Yates was cautious and said that their drilling rig was removed, to be followed by tests to determine "what kind of producer it will be."

The BLM problems, compounded or alleviated by FLPMA depending on your viewpoint, were treated in Chapter 10. Although there were yet no BLM Wildernesses, they had Wilderness Study Areas within their purview. Some of those areas do contain considerable amounts of strippable coal and are near enough to large power plants in the northwestern parts of the state to be economically attractive. Consequently, although the areas are now national Wilderness, the issue of mining in them will be treated here. The situation may evolve into the need for a legislative solution. The courts are already involved.

A very simplified version of the complex sets of problems in only one small area under BLM jurisdiction is developed to illustrate the precursory events leading to a possible wilderness legislative conclusion. The four districts of BLM in the state, using a Wilderness Inventory Handbook, (starting in 1978) plunged into a three-phased program of wilderness study. The phases were 1: Initial and Intensive Inventory, 2: Study of Wilderness Study Areas (WSA), and 3: Reporting through the Secretary and the President to Congress against a deadline of October 21, 1991. The Albuquerque District identified 57 roadless areas in 1978. Thirty-five of the areas were not recommended for intensive inventory and 22 were. Of those 22, three were selected as WSAs after accelerated studies. Signals changed in 1979 and another area was dropped from further wilderness consideration. So 18 out of the 22 were subjected to intensive inventory. Half of those areas survived and were recommended for WSA status. Three areas were selected as (immediate) "Instant Study Areas" (ISAs). One was near, but not in the Albuquerque District. It is a large lava flow southeast of Grants called the El Malpais Natural Area.

Three areas in the northwestern part of the Albuquerque District that did rise quickly in the accelerated inventory process are the 3,520 acre Bisti, the 19,000 acre De-na-zin, and the 6,000 acre Ah-she-sle-pah. Public meetings were held to attempt to obtain as much useful information about the areas as possible from that source. It was immediately discovered that the three WSAs had unique rock and weathered formations unlike any other comparable areas. They have cultural (archaeological) and paleontological resources uncovered by erosion processes. There are many other areas in the vicinity that have similar cultural and paleo resources but they are not as extensively uncovered. The Bisti WSA, however, is such a badland that it has prevented a comprehensive inventory of such resources. This is part of the attraction to the public.

There is an industry proposal for a Coal Preference Right Lease Application (PRLA) that involves leasing of 75,510 acres of public, Indian, state, and private lands underlaid by federal coal. Such coal deposits underlay much of the three WSAs. About 22,000 acres would be strip mined and 26,650 acres mined by underground methods.

Another factor is a proposed New Mexico Generating Station (NMGS). It is proposed to be located on a site near the edge of the Bisti WSA. A Sunbelt Mining Company and an Arch Minerals Company own coal reserves adjacent to the NMGS site. The generating station would require 35,000 acre feet of water for wet-cooling towers. The storage reservoir would be formidable in the middle of the desert along the right of way for a couple of 36-inch pipelines. Then there must be the inevitable powerlines and some railroad haulage lines.

In 1961, long before WSA consideration, the BLM issued two federal coal leases to Sunbelt Mining. The 1978-79 BLM inventory identified a part of lease land as the Bisti WSA, with much public support. Congress passed a Public Law 96-475 on October 19, 1980 for the Interior Secretary to issue federal coal leases outside the Bisti WSA to compensate for the loss to the leasee.

A draft "Proposed Wilderness Areas Environmental Impact Statement" issued November 30, 1982 contains a summary proposal. "The BLM proposes the designation of the approximately 19,922 acre De-na-zin WSA. The BLM also proposes the approximately 6, 563 acre Ah-shi-sle-pah WSA be designated as non-wilderness." Deadline for review by the public was April 8, 1983.

One other consideration which BLM attempts to keep in mind as they try to solve the complicated puzzle: the Secretary of Interior, in

April 1982, established a leasing target of 1.2 to 1.5 billion tons of in-place federal coal for lease sale in September 1983, for the San Juan River Region in which the three WSAs are located.

The state of New Mexico owns a Section 32 which is the virtual gateway of the Bisti WSA. The Sunbelt Mining Company has a lease on that 640 acre section. The Sierra Club Legal Foundation has made an appeal in which three issues predominate. The first is that the state laws requiring restoration after mining to the original condition cannot be met. The State Land Office and Sunbelt Mining claim that the original use is grazing. There are reports which state that the grazing capacity is zero, as is the forage capacity. The Sierra Club claims the real use is scenic wilderness and recreational and that the restoration after stripmining the area to such a real use condition is impossible.

The second issue is that there are state regulations defining Public Parks and that the Bisti WSA qualfies under that definition. The regulations further say that mining cannot take place adjacent to such a public park area without approval of the owner, in this case the BLM. No such request has been submitted by Sunbelt.

A third issue is one of due process in which the State Land Office is one of the parties in opposition to the Sierra Club. Yet the Land Office is one of the agents sitting in judgment of the appeal. Consequently we have the strange situation in which the accused is the judge. The whole set of issues is yet to be decided.

The Lame Duck Session of Congress adjourned for the year at Christmas time, 1982. Secretary Watt thereupon announced that he was withdrawing more than 99,000 acres of wilderness study areas in New Mexico and similar amounts in other states. The 3,500 acre Bisti Badlands were removed from the BLM list along with thirteen other WSAs in New Mexcio. On December 10, 1982, the House Public Lands Subcommittee held a hearing at which Watt's authority to remove WSAs from the list was questioned. The Wilderness Society stated that it planned to file a suit to block Watt's decision.

Within a few days after Watt's "hit list" was announced, the public outcry was so great that the BLM, at the urging of Senator Domenici, reestablished the Bisti as a WSA. PNM, the Public Service Co. of New Mexico, also claimed they were for a Bisti Wilderness Area all along and that they were willing, temporarily, to trade their coal leases in the WSA for other leases in less sensitive areas.

Our new Congressman Bill Richardson arranged a House Interior and Insular Affairs Committee Hearing in Santa Fe on May 21, 1983. Over three hundred people attended the hearing. The testimony was dominantly for wilderness enactment of the three Bisti areas.

Freshman Senator Bingaman was also in attendance.

A Senate Bill was introduced by Senator Bingaman on August 3, 1983 entitled "San Juan Basin Wilderness Protection Act of 1983." Rep. Richardson co-sponsored the bill on his side of the Congress. The areas mentioned are 3,968 acres of the Bisti, 23,872 acres of the De-na-zin, and 7,193 acres of the Ah-shi-sle-pah. Also, 2,720 acres of the Fossil Forest are included to be withdrawn from mineral entry to prevent surface disturbance and to permit paleontological study, evacuation, and interpretation.

Secretary Watt said on January 9, 1983 that he loves wilderness and that he would not think of taking advantage of the three month "window of opportunity" to issue mining and drilling leases in enacted Wildernesses before the deadline in the Wilderness Act controls. He said that he "had a wonderful year" in office but that some of the conservationists' statements about him were highly disturbing.

There is one consideration not given in any of the Environmental Impact Statements in the San Juan Basin which I think is quite important. Burning coal in power plants to produce energy has been the only concern or use anticipated for the coal. The use of coal as a chemical feed stock for the future may be a much higher use in the national interest. Materials synthesized out of such chemical feed stocks may be our salvation when the critical mineral supplies fail us. Should we not reserve some for those uses?

We do have a dependence on foreign materials in the form of critical minerals. The following chart gives some measure of the degrees of dependence.

TABLE
U.S. Import Dependence, Selected Minerals
(Imports as percent of Apparent Consumption)

	1950	1970	1978	1979	1980
Bauxite[1]	71	80	93	93	94
Chromium	100	100	91	90	91
Cobalt	92	96		94	93
Copper	35	8	20	12	14
Iron ore	5	30	29	25	22
Lead	59	40	9	4	[2]
Manganese	77	94	97	98	97
Nickel	99	91	80	69	73
Platinum	91	98	90	89	87
Tungsten	80	40	56	58	54
Zinc	37	60	66	63	58

[1] 1978,1979,1980 includes alumina.
[2] Net export.
SOURCE: 1950, 1970, *Report of National Commission on Material Policy*, June 1973, pp. 2-23; 1976-80. *Mineral Commodity Summaries 1981*, Bureau of Mines, U.S. Dept. of the Interior.

Our lame duck Senator Schmitt's father was the originator of the "Overthrust Belt Theory" of mineral activity. Many Wildernesses are in the mountains along the overthrust belt and thus subject to suspicions of undiscovered mineral wealth.

Most of the ore bodies and mineral reserves are privately owned and have been for many decades. Some of the public lands have been "blessed" with some low-grade mineral deposits and some have not been carefully inventoried by private industry because of easier access to better valued ones under their own control. The state has been receiving severence taxes for years for fortuitous coal, oil, and gas withdrawals from state lands. There is some question about the accounting-reporting system of withdrawals of publicly-owned mineral resources. Federal land, on the other hand, does not require royalties or severance taxes.

Although allowed by the Wilderness Act, mining in National Wilderness had been far from prevalent. It has been easier and more economical to mine outside of wilderness because it is less rugged country. That is not to say that the prospectors have been lazy. Very few economical or commercial grade finds have been made in Wilderness. In our own state, as in many of the western states, the amount of Wilderness is small, less than two percent of the area (see end of Chapter 7).

Admittedly, mining (paydirt) strikes do not follow very regular statistical area distribution rules. If they did, we could expect about two percent of our finds to be on National Wilderness. If one were buying mining stocks in Wilderness, then, it would not be a winning proposition.

There is an Appendix-Mineral Resources, at the back of this book. It has little to do with the wilderness legislation dilemma per se, but it does consider some of the probabilities of future findings in our RARE conflict studies. It was submitted as part of the information which the administration and our congressmen received in support of our RARE II recommendations. If you are interested in mining in New Mexico, you might browse through it.

CHAPTER 13
Epilogue

T he dilemma of wilderness, the paradox, the enigma of undeveloped public land has been addressed in previous chapters. Perhaps U.S. National Wilderness Areas may generate more problems for people than they solve. That evaluation may be weighted in whatever direction the person most affected wants it to be. The dimensions of the dilemma, the paradox, and the enigma have been described, possibly too briefly for those more searching minds to find satisfaction. An academic approach to the subject might reveal solution paths to each of the problems. Wilderness managers could give you their versions.

There are a number of man's problems which a far flung National Wilderness system cannot begin to address. Famine is not a part of the dilemma. The entire cycle of drought induced famines can be influenced to a lesser degree by the capability of the wilderness to improve the capacities of the watersheds. The wildlife in wilderness cannot long sustain the human food chain. The wilderness characteristics are not conducive to even marginal agriculture. The sanctuary of wilderness has attracted some illegal and covert agriculture such as growing marijuana in forested areas seldom visited by what these growers consider as interlopers.

Pestilence is not promoted by wilderness. For example, even bubonic plague requires a human vector in its cycle. Fleas on rodents have to acquire the bubonic factor from man. The black rat which propagates in human garbage has long been suspected as carrying the fleas to squirrels and other rodents on the suburban fringes. New Mexico has had several cases per year of the pneumonic plague variety. Children seem to be the most frequently affected. Childish curiosity drawing them to dead squirrels has been identified in several cases. Pets have sometimes provided a logical connector between rodents and humans. Burrowing owls have been suspected of conducting fleas from one rodent colony to another. In any of these events, the existence of National Wilderness does not appear to be a cause of bubonic or pneumonic plague.

War, the white horse of the Apocalypse, surely is not promoted by wilderness although some day those nations that have wilderness may cause the have-not nations to covet it. Historically, the Huns and Visigoths descended upon the southwestern European countries because their own environments became unliveable. Crop failures and famine drove them to more moderate climes.

Strife, the red horse of the Apocalypse, appears to be running again in the forms of terrorism. It does not originate in wilderness, although outlaws have had strongholds in remote areas off the trade routes. Ladron Peak, in New Mexico, was a longstanding wilderness sanctuary for the robbers who waylaid the freight wagon trains along the Old Spanish Trail, El Camino Real. The dilemma of wilderness has not yet caused classic strife, but that is not to say that it might not generate some minor strife in lawful societies. The noise of aircraft flying over and in Grand Canyon could drive some wilderness nuts to the point of shooting the offending aircraft.

Over-population is one of the adverse vectors of wilderness because it tends to increase the abuses described in Chapter 2.

In our Southwest, illegal pot hunters have rifled archaeological and anthropological sites in the public lands, including National Wilderness.

Poaching of big game animals is not dominant in National Wilderness because it is far from roads and generally not good ORV country. However, there is some poaching in some de facto wilderness areas.

The cutting of live pinon trees has approached epidemic proportions in our southwest National Forests and some BLM areas. It takes as much as three hundred years for a pinon to grow to maturity. We are far beyond the sustained yield point in the harvest. Wilderness margins have been invaded by live wood cutters near the roadheads. Many of the trailheads have been disfigured by such mindless firewood harvesting. The roadless National Wilderness Areas tend to protect the forest against such green pinon cutting practices. Most Wilderness Areas are poor tree farms in any case.

The final dilemma may be that of access for the public. As more of the public has time and energy to spend on outdoor recreation, they find more ways to do it, including going to Wilderness Areas. The neophyte, going into a Wilderness for the first time is often insensitive to the wilderness condition and can commit several transgressions unwittingly. Good wilderness manners are not instantaneously acquired. If there is only one way to get into a specific wilderness through one principal roadhead, the wilderness manager has a problem, that of concentrated overuse of the trails leading from that trailhead. So he attempts to develop additional access points to spread out the use.

At that juncture, the manager runs into a host of problems generic to access to public lands. The land development process has surrounded the public lands like an ocean around an island. So few western cities have been fortunate enough to have National Wilderness Areas immediately adjacent to and abutting their city limits. Soon, if not in advance of enactment, houses are backed up to the Wilderness boundary. Wilderness users have been known to crawl across the fence to get into and out of the Wilderness area. Cars are parked along the streets and in some instances, in front of driveways to the consternation of the house occupants. Shortly, the wilderness manager wants to solve the problem by putting a parking lot inside the National Forest (or other agency) Wilderness to accommodate the wilderness users. That works for a little while until the teenagers discover the neat parking lot and start having beer-busts late in the nights with loud stereos and trash accumulations. The next step, after the homeowners object to the attractive nuisance, is to close the parking lot at ten o'clock in the evening. The wilderness users arrive later to discover that they cannot get their cars out of the parking lot.

Another access problem to the public lands, including Wilderness, is evident when the land manager wants to improve an old road across a privately owned ranch to allow better access to the public land. The rancher may, and often does, object. He puts up a locked gate. If he does not, the public comes in, leaves trash, leaves the gates open, and sometimes vandalizes the fences or runs ORVs all over his land. They even sometimes shoot his cattle or leave a bar of soap in one of his water tanks.

The rancher throws up his hands and locks his gates. The wilderness manager is in a dilemma. How can he solve this problem?

The public has a real problem with knowing where the boundaries of public lands are, and what regulations apply. The Gramm-Rudman Act of 1986 has reduced and even eliminated field personnel so access controls are practically eliminated also. Perhaps the only answer lies in increased signing of boundaries and increased public education programs by the public land agencies. Volunteers could put up the signs if asked.

APPENDIX
MINERAL RESOURCES

Atlantic Richfield Company Summary of RARE II Conflicts

A tlantic Richfield Company is extremely concerned about the escalation in the rate of federal land withdrawals from multiple public use. Besides the Roadless Area Review and Evaluation, the Alaska National Interest Lands Act (Alaska d(2) lands) presently being considered by Congress, the Wilderness Review by the Bureau of Land Management (BLM) are examples of procedures that will have long-term consequences for the availability of energy and mineral resources in the United States. Such withdrawals obviously limit federal acreage accessible for energy and mineral exploration and development. And, most lands under investigation for withdrawal contain minerals as well as geological structures favorable to oil and gas.

Besides protecting wilderness values, the federal government is obliged to consider development of energy and mineral resources. Reconciling these conflicting goals can only be achieved by a balanced assessment of important lands decisions in terms of multiple long-range national interests. Unfortunately, such objectivity is often foregone, either because of the lack of adequate energy and mineral data, or failure to analyze it properly.

Placing lands into the "Further Planning" category may produce additional information on surface resources such as timber and potential for recreational uses. But, no provision is made for the evaluation of subsurface values. Thus, for energy and mineral resources, the "Further Planning" regulations are, in fact, more stringent than indicated in the Wilderness Act itself. Atlantic Richfield Company believes that sound public land allocation decisions must include a complete evaluation of the energy and minerals resource potentials involved as well as other uses. Public land policies which prevent energy and mineral investigation block knowledge of potential, vital resources. Therefore, RARE II inventoried lands with known or suspected potential for energy and mineral resources must not be given "Wilderness" or "Further Planning" classifications.

The attached information concerning RARE II reflects a summary of areas of concern that our Company has with regard to areas recommended for withdrawal in the Final Environmental Statement on RARE II. Included are maps of eight Western states which identify conflict areas for energy and mineral resources. Items differentiating resources potential classifications as (1) degree of favorable potential for sizeable accumulations and (2) the perceived economic viability for development under current conditions. Over time, further investigation and exploration into these areas — and/or changes in economics — could alter the importance of the roadless areas.

Additional data with regard to energy and mineral resource potential for specific RARE II tracts are available in our submittal to the Forest Service on the Draft Environmental Statement September 29, 1978.

FINAL ENVIRONMENTAL STATEMENT CONFLICT AREAS BY STATE RARE II

tate: NEW MEXICO

CONFLICTS

ract umber	Area Name	Desig- nation	1,000 Acres	Base Metals	Uranium	Oil/Gas	Geotl
)08	Ryan Hill	FP	37	Critical			
)11	Withington	W	19	Critical			
)13	Apache Kid	W	132	Critical	Critical		
)31	Latir Peak	W	26	Critical		Critical	
3032	Columbine-Hondo	FP	46	Critical		Critical	
3033	Wheeler Peak	W	15	Critical		Critical	
B3038	Pecos Wild	W	77	Critical		Critical	
/H3038	Pecos Wild	FP	18	Critical		Critical	
3069	Capitan Mountains	W	38	Critical		Critical	
3070	White Mountains	W	38	Critical		Critical	
3070	White Mountains	FP	1	Critical		Critical	
)72	W. Face Sacramento Mts.	FP	42	Critical		Critical	
)74	Little Dog & Pup Canyons	FP	26			Significant	
)77	S. Guadalupe Mountains	W	21			Critical	
l02	Polvadera	FP	15	Critical		Moderate	
3156	Contiguous to Gila	W	1	Critical		Moderate	
3162	Contiguous to Black & Aldo	W	34	Critical			

98

Comments by Corry McDonald in March 1979
on Atlantic Richfield Co. RARE II Conflicts
FS Wilderness Areas Recommended

A gainst the background of RARE II, N.M. RARE II Statistics (see Chapter 7).

The concern of Atlantic Richfield in New Mexico rings with a hollow note. It does seem strange that without core drilling, the specific .6% of our State, or 5% of our National Forest recommended for Wilderness becomes so important in the overall balance.

A&R has selected ten areas recommended for Wilderness as being critical for base metals. Let us examine these areas in the light of the past and recent eagerness of the mining industry to freely use and explore these areas.

Withington contains no operating mines or prospects in 1979. The only active mining area near the Withington Roadless Area was at Rosedale, a small mining town that existed from 1882 to 1937. The gold and silver lead was composed of broken stringers which were mined painstakingly over the years to produce a total of approximately $300,000. All that remains is the tailings since the buildings and larger structures were removed in the late 1950's and early 1960's.

A few prospect holes exist around the lower reaches of Mt. Withington. An outcropping of galena in Bear Trap Canyon has been periodically scratched at by prospectors over the centuries. Some fluoride appears to be associated with the galena. Potato Canyon has some pieces of selenium float mixed in with extensive weathered smithsonite and shale fragments. Here again is a mountain with some evidences of mineralization around its lower reaches outside the roadless area apparently without sufficient economic quantities to induce development or much notable assessment.

Apache Kid in the southern San Mateo mountains has been scoured by prospectors for well over a century without producing any records of discoveries of note. Some of the steep canyons on the west side show some chunks of limestone with veinlets of cuprite. The theory that the Green Cananea-Bisbee rift northeastward through the Black Range and San Mateos appears to be far fetched. Some pitchblende and sphalerite mixed with iron pyrites were observed on a trail northwest of Blue Mountain. A broken ore sack on a mule or burro may have been the source. We met a prospector on the ridge above Springtime Campground in the mid-1960's who claimed to have found about $25 worth of wire silver "several years ago" up near Vick's Peak. He was still looking in 1971. The old Pankey mine dumps indicate to the casual onlooker that some gold and silver ores were mined without much success at that small scale.

The suspicion that uranium could occur in vein deposits in the Apache Kid massif is possibly credible. The value of such vein deposits throughout the State as compared to the peneconcordant deposits should not attract AR or any large company. The USGS does not seem to be very impressed by the prospects.

Latir Peak in Taos County is indicated as critical for base metals and oil and gas by the AR conflict statement. The nearness of the Molycorp mine near Questa may be painting the whole region in false colors. Flag Mountain to the southeast of Questa has been drilled by Molycorp and claims have been filed. Only one hole was drilled in the area surrounding the Latir area and that was somewhere west of Pinabeta Peak, apparently without any showings.

Some of the trails in the central canyons do show some scattered evidences of secondary mineralization. The Baldy Mountain south face above Cabresto Creek does have some more extensive mineralized fault zones exposed. The extensive rockslides in the Latir Roadless Area do not show much mineralization. The Sangre de Cristos upthrust of Precambrian rocks would tend to indicate a series of horizons for the pegmatite minerals but the Latir Areas has not shown any recorded. The Cedros prospect on the Castillo Land Grand and a showing near Lobo Peak to the north and south have shown feldspar-rich pegmatites which may contain concentrations of other minerals deeper in the veins.

In the upper reaches of the Rito del Medio, an access road was dozed into a uranium claim that was a small vein deposit. We again have a disfiguring "road" to a non-producing claim.

The nearest oil or gas well was drilled in 1960 in the Las Vegas

Basin to the east. It and the coal deposits in the Vermejo Ranch area probably influenced Pennzoil to buy the ranch. However, it does not make much economic sense to prospect for either oil or gas in the Precambrian rocks at the high altitude of the Latir Peaks Roadless Area. The AR statement of "Critical" for Oil/Gas on Latir Peak must be a mistake. The USGS Report says "Precambrian — no potential."

The old mines along the western escarpment (called the Archer Mining District) must have been tantalizing to the miners in the 1880 era. The vein materials looked better than the Elizabethtown-Baldy lodes (much as did the Bull-O-The-Woods deposits on top of the mountain above Twining) but they could not pay their way to the distant smelters of that day a century ago. Possibly a large volume drift/stope mining operation at about the elevation of the forest boundary west of Venado Peak might pay off if anyone could figure out a compatible mill flow-sheet and smeltering process. The operations at Twining failed with even better ore. In any event, a mine at such low levels would not affect the surface Wilderness above.

Wheeler Peak Contiguous Area is rated by AR as critical for both base metals and Oil/Gas. The USGS report also says "Precambrian — No potential" for Oil/Gas. Who would drill for oil and gas at 11000-13000 ft. elevation? In granite?

There are two old mines in the South Fork area west of the Taos Ski Basin (Williams Fork of the Hondo). One was up on the ridge south of the present Taos East Condominiums and the other one is up at the head of the South Fork where the stream comes out of the rockslides. Both gold and silver in the primary and secondary forms have been found in the Wheeler Area but there is no record of any appreciable quantities taken out other than at the Amizette mines and placers. The placer gold values kept the hopes fired up while Twining paid out about $300,000 for the smelter near the head of the Arroyo Hondo in 1897-98. He probably made part of his money by backing some of the Elizabethtown placer operations.

The Twining fault line surfaces on the west face of Kachina Peak at about the 11500 foot elevation level. A drift mining operation was attempted three separate times in the 1890's, only to be wiped out by snowslides and unstable ground. One can imagine that the lode was washed down South Fork Creek over the ages. Generations of placer miners have scraped the bedrock the whole distance to the Rio Grande since 1897 — without much notoriety.

The Ski Area has been the real bonanza. A completely undeveloped watershed is probably the highest use of the whole area.

Pecos Wilderness Contiguous Areas again are underlaid by

Precambrian granite so the chances for Oil/Gas are "none" according the the USGS.

There is a small chance that another Pecos mine with its complex mixture of zinc, lead, and copper sulfides, including minor amounts of silver and gold, may be discovered some day in the jumbled Precambrian schists, diabase, granite, and related igneous rocks of the areas surrounding the Pecos Wilderness. That hope has kept an active interest alive since the Pecos Mine shut down in 1939. Teams from four large mining companies have combed the areas without filing any new claims in the last forty years. Three claims have been filed by individual prospectors but they are not being currently worked.

The mica mine on Elk Mountain might well be reopened if some new use for mica would raise its price to mineable levels. It is on the edge of one of our proposed wilderness additions to the Pecos.

Capitan Mountain Area is considered by AR to be critical for both base metals and oil/gas. The potential for oil/gas, according to the USGS, is low on the basis of the fact that the mountain is a large boulder batholith with extensive intrusions. There is some coal at a low horizon (5000 ft. lower than the top of Capitan Peak) about ten miles south of the escarpment. The coal is bituminous, quite good quality but the beds are broken up by igneous dikes and sills. It is not very probable that the coal deposits continue under the mountain because the batholith that formed the mountain appears to have broken through the earlier coal horizon.

Back to the oil/gas potential again, but only to point out that Capitan Mountain is well south of the perimeter of the Pedernal Land Mass and northeast of the Orogrande Basin. The closest oil/gas well to the mountain was about forty miles east (not far from Roswell) and it turned to carbon dioxide and brackish water before it could be brought into production.

There was a small uranium deposit in an vein complex on the north foothills of Capitan Mountain. The discovery, shortly after 1900, was disappointing to the prospectors who were looking for gold and silver. Subsequent relocation of the prospect in about 1960 was not followed by any mining or claim refiling. There is a Thorium Canyon in which two old claims were staked. The canyon is outside the Forest Service's Roadless Area A3069. There appears to be no record of any ore being produced. The thorite is in several "irregular veins of highly irregular grades" according to the USGS.

The rock glaciers high up on the sides of Capitan Mountain are an outstanding geological feature but they appear to have no economic value at all.

While it is true that the mountain has a wide variety of jumbled veins and brecciated zones showing smatterings of some mineralization, there have been no commercial operations developed anywhere on the mountain. An old wagon road goes up Pancho Canyon on the southwest side of the mountains to the bottom of the rockslide in the vicinity of several prospect holes at that elevation. Some brown stained quartz was dropped on the overgrown old road in mute testimony of someone's dream! Even the east-west strike of the mountain has no clear reason but has intrigued geologists for years. Possibly AR can solve the mountain's secret. However there does not appear to be enough public evidence to justify their assessment of the "Critical" for base metals and oil/gas.

White Mountain Contiguous Area, of 20,700 acres, is the roadless area generally east of the existing White Mountain National Wilderness. The AR conflict statement has the A&B prefix numbers reversed.

Reversing the usual order, the supposed "Critical" conflict statement made by AR appears to be contrary to the USGS summary. The entire area has been rated by that agency as of low potential for gas and oil although no recorded wells have been driven for that purpose in that area or vicinity. The basic geology of the area is that of volcanic batholiths containing intrusions of Tertiary magmas. If there was any oil/gas bearing formations beforehand, the massive uplifts forming the Sierra Blanca range probably disrupted it. Drilling explorations around the perimeter may someday provide more certain knowledge but drilling in the upper parts of the basaltic masses probably will be counterproductive.

On the contrary, some drilling for base metals has been done in the vicinity. A molybdenum prospect on the southern edge of the area was permitted, including an access road or "travelway" as some are now known, in the late 1960's. A shaft was driven and subsequently caved in and the road bladed closed. There must have been inadequate ore.

The Nogal mines just outside the National Forest Boundary to the northwest did produce some 13,000 ounces of gold out of stringers and veins in monzonite porphyry and andesite. The hills within the National Forest have been riddled with prospect holes and some short drifts in a vain attempt to prolong the life of the District while there were still miners and equipment in the vicinity. There are some old claims in the Church, Indian, Bonito, and Betsy additions within the B3070 area. No active mining is occurring within these additions at present. Some of the claims along Tortolito Creek were placers although the original claims were filed in the expectation of finding the lode on them.

The most probable areas of basic metal occurrence are those in the A3070 areas to the north and west of the Wilderness Area. These are discussed in the Further Planning Section of these comments.

Southern Guadalupe Mountains Area is rated by AR as critical for oil/gas. The Forest Service rates the potential oil/gas as high. It is in the Delaware Basin, the most highly producing oil/gas area in the U.S. We have mapped corridors into the few drilling sites in the area. The Indian Lake Gas Field is about 25 miles west of the town of Carlsbad and about 30 miles north of the Guadalupe Ridge. The entire Guadalupe Ridge is so interesting geologically, not only because it is a major barrier reef, that the geologists use it as a virtual textbook. Much of the AR capital originated in the oil and gas fields to the north about 40 miles from Carlsbad. They are obviously knowledgeable about the potential of the Forest Service roadless area even if the deep drilling exploration has not been very extensive. The Delaware Basin oil/gas producing horizon in the Southern Guadalupe Area is about 8000 feet, approximately that under the original Anderson* location to the northeast. In any event, wells would probably not be sited on the reef top or on the southern escarpment of the ridge. Dark Canyon is a more logical location from a surface feature vantage point. Wilderness enactment would not be that crucial to the AR interests.

Gila Wilderness Contiguous Areas have been hopefully combed by prospectors since the Santa Rita original discoveries. Most of the copper discoveries are out east of the Black Range (Copper Flat, for example). The southwestern pieces closest to Silver City do have showings of copper, silver, gold, and tellurium. The histories of these claims are well known, having been through many owners' hands and generally unsuccessfully. These fragments could be omitted from the Gila Contiguous Areas without much total area loss.

The areas do contain some fluorspar deposits from which commercial shipments have been made in the past. Old wagon roads (since impassable) once led to some shallow tunnels whose dumps currently still show the typical purple stains. The Burro Mountain deposits and others outside the Contiguous Areas are much stronger deposits. Consequently, there does not appear to be adequate economic reason to exclude the limited areas from wilderness enactment on their marginal fluorspar potentials.

The AR enlistment says moderate potential for oil/gas. The extensive volcanism has so far stopped any exploratory drilling for oil/gas

---

*R.O. Anderson was Atlantic Richfield Chairman (until 1985).

in the Contiguous Areas. Perhaps someone can find a soft spot one of these years. It may happen when someone is doing some geothermal drilling. The geology of the area does not hold much promise for oil and gas, however.

Aldo Leopold or Black Range Contiguous Areas have been probed by generations of miners. The northwest corner of the Primitive Area has shown good panned samples of tin with traces of gold and silver in the rhyolite country rock. The Carpenter District southwest of the Primitive Area has a history of some open pit tin mining by means of gas shovel, dragline and sinker. The shipments to the El Paso Smelter were sporadic, supposedly because the smelting process used was not compatible with the associated gangues. The records imply heavy penalties for some of the shipments after which hand sorting was resorted to prior to shutdown.

American Smelting and Refining representatives have testified in one of the several Forest Service Hearings that the Black Range might overlay massive copper deposits. We have long thought that the Robert O. Anderson acquisitions of the ranch lands to the east of the Black Range were for more reason than ranching. Although the extent of the Copper Flat low grade deposits probably would not warrant much open pit mining, the area would lend itself to a deep shaft away from the eastern edge of the Kneeling Nun Tuff formations. The Bureau of Mines Geological Survey Bulletin 1319-E indicates that the volcanic rocks of Tertiary age have an aggregate maximum thickness of nearly 17,000 feet. It goes on to say that the volcanic sequence at any one place is probably less than 7,000 feet. Consequently a shaft of 5500 or 600 feet could provide the horizon for exploratory drifts under the Black Range massif to determine if high grade copper values were present. They would have to be high to justify the high mining costs. Does AR want to take such a risk?

Re: FURTHER PLANNING Areas, AR COMMENTS

A R has indicated six areas recommended for *Further Planning* as being critical for base metals. Let us examine these areas in the light of past and recent eagerness of the mining industry to freely use and explore these areas.

Ryan Hill has had the Kelly Mine producing for years, *outside* the roadless area. It has played out. The mining costs have overtaken the return. There have been many small mines around the periphery of the mountain in the past. None of them are working now. Last fall a miner drove a bulldozer up onto his claim near the top of Copper Canyon and constructed a road. The decision to permit the road is being appealed. He thinks that he can use the dozer to remove a rockslide to uncover gold bearing ore underneath. If the miner (Mr. Kempton) has the same success with his claim as all of the previous generations of miners have had on Ryan Hill, we will have a disqualifiying road to another non-producing mine. We are in extremely poor condition as a nation if we have to rely upon Ryan Hill for our critical metal supply. I have seen a manganese prospect (abandoned) on the south side of North Baldy. The haulage was too expensive and the lead was too spotty. Barite has been mined commercially in Water Canyon outside the roadless area. The Kelly and Iron Mask mines also have barite deposits. The quality and quantity are only marginally competitive.

Perhaps if AR were to sink a shaft in the vicinity of the Mule Shoe ranch foothills and run exploratory drifts under the mountain, something of value might be discovered. Possibly a few drill holes put down in the roaded area near Langmuir Lab could give them the necessary encouragement to spend the multimillions required to mine the mountain mass on a successful economic scale. Such a mining method would not affect the surface wilderness values.

Columbine-Hondo had had a mottled mining history. There has been some relatively successful mining (Caribel Mine) during the days of the stamp mill there. Every generation of prospectors has combed every canyon and ridge for its bonanza. The shaft mine on Gold Hill went through two sets of owners and broke them. The mine just above Red River to the south (near the ski run) occupied about eight men for several years with generally uninteresting results. A mine in the Deer Creek Canyon caved in on a sourdough miner early in the century.

The feldspar-rich pegmatite prospect pit near Lobo Peak must have been frustrating because it was so far from a compatible smelter. Even today it would probably not be able to justify the transportation costs. It surely is not a critical mineral.

The extensive drilling conducted by Molycorp on Flag Mountain does tend to indicate that they have the molybdenum horizon well mapped out. Our NMWSC boundary excludes the area which should be required for that mining. The disfigurement of the west face of Flag Mountain will be some kind of a monument to man's necessity. Hopefully the Columbine Creek drainage will not be damaged by ground-water migration from the Flag Mountain disturbances. It is part of a very valuable watershed.

Quite possibly, long after all of the red bed copper deposits in the southwestern part of the State are mined out at much lower costs, the shear zones along the Red River could yield some replacement deposits, but at comparatively miniscule quantities and gargantuan costs.

It is almost too bad that the Wilderness Act requires the Secretaries of Agriculture and Interior to assess the mineral and natural resource values ad infinitum in existing wilderness because it has been so futile in the Columbine-Hondo area. So many fortunes have been squandered in trying to develop the gold and silver leads in the Precambrian granites. The closest anyone came to a real killing was in the main mines of the Twining area but the ore froze up twice in the smelting process in a surprisingly sophisticated smelter and mill. Someone will someday give it another try. The ante now is probably at least ten million dollars to treat the first one hundred tons. However, the Bull-O-The-Woods ore does look extrememly good. It is outside our proposed Wilderness Area. Can AR afford the gamble?

The AR indication that the Columbine-Hondo area is "Critical" for Oil/Gas is no more than a shot in the dark. The USGS Report says "Precambrian — No potential."

The USFS indicated "Further PLanning" for some other reason(s) than meets the eye. There does not seem to be anything in public record to indicate justification. Perhaps some of the tourist public wants to continue to ride trail bikes and snowmobiles in the area. There is already much area northeast of Red River for those purposes.

White Mountain Wilderness Additions (A3070) named Pine, Water, and Horse, are approximately 980 acres. The probability of oil/gas in these additions appear to be even more improbable than on the other side of the mountain.

The Water Canyon mineralization is quite promising, as the base mineral showings are in the Pine and Horse additions. After considerably more analysis, the Forest Service may well decide that Wilderness is not the correct recommendation for this set of small additions. Perhaps AR could show enough interest in these areas to assess the full worth of these small areas. Maybe they are "critical" areas, but not according to current information recorded.

West Face Sacramento Mountain Area exposes a western edge of the Permian Basin beyond any previous oil/gas discoveries. The Precambrian border and the thin Paleozoic sections are complicated by the upthrust to a sufficient degree to discourage any exploration for oil and gas up until the present. Some drilling in the foothills has been done by companies usually interested in copper and silver but no mining followed their probings. A retired miner that lived in La Luz in the 1950's told me that he worked in most of the mines around there and saw scattered small pockets of galena broken up by subsequent faulting. That is probably characteristic of the area's mineralization. Consequently if the area is critical for oil/gas and base metals, we are in bad shape.

Little Dog and Pup Area in Otero County is rated as "significant" by AR for Oil/Gas. The area is on the west side of the Guadalupe Mountains west of Carlsbad. Geologically the area is outside of the western edge of the Delaware Basin. A couple of dry holes deeper than 20,000 feet have been drilled. The Guadalupe Mountain Uplift complicated the establishment of a clear structural picture of the basement rocks. Perhaps AR meant "significantly uninteresting."

Polvadera Peak Area in southern Rio Arriba County is rated as critical for base metals and moderate for oil/gas by AR. Some pumice and its possible geothermal horizon potential is present but it is surely more abundant in the adjacent areas if someone wanted to put up the development money. These prospects are surely not base metals although they touch upon an energy source. The other indication of moderate potential for oil/gas is probably realistic on the basis that a well near Abiqui in the canyon to the north of the Peak produced showings of natural gas containing a predominance (96.5%) of carbon dioxide. It does seem that drilling the mountain would be quite uneconomical compared to sinking wells several thousands of feet lower down at the surfaces of the valleys and canyons.

REFERENCES

INTRODUCTION

1. Colbert, Edwin H. "Mammoths and Men," *Natural History Magazine*, New York: The American Museum of Natural History, 1940.
2. Wernick, Robert. "Sagas Are Still Alive and Kicking for Icelanders," *Smithsonian Magazine*. Washington, D.C., Smithsonian Associates, January, 1986.
3. McDonald, Corry. *Wilderness, A New Mexico Legacy*. Santa Fe, NM: Sunstone Press, 1985.
4. *Ibid.*

CHAPTER 3

1. Viorst, Milton. *Outsider in the Senate, Senator Clinton P. Anderson's Memoirs*. New York: World Publishing Co., 1970.

CHAPTER 5

1. Klein, Richard M. "The Florence Floods," *Natural History Magazine*. New York: The American Museum of Natural History, 1969.
2. Watt, Kenneth E.F. "Man's Efficient Rush Towards Deadly Dullness," *Natural History Magazine*, New York: The American Museum of Natural History, 1972.

CHAPTER 6

1. "Administrative Policies for the National Parks and Monuments of Scientific Significance" (Natural Area Category), U.S. Dept. of Interior, National Park Service, U.S. Printing Office, (Revised 1970).
2. McDonald, Corry, *Wilderness, A New Mexico Legacy*. Santa Fe, NM: Sunstone Press, 1985.

BIBLIOGRAPHY

Northrop, Stuart A. *Minerals of New Mexico.* New Mexico University Bulletin No. 379, Geological Survey, Vol. 6, No. 1. Albuquerque, NM: University of New Mexico, 1944.

_____. *Minerals of New Mexico.* (revised edition). Albuquerque, NM: University of New Mexico Press, 1959.

Jones, Fayette A. *Old New Mexico Mines and Minerals.* Santa Fe, NM: New Mexico Printing Co., 1904.

Eriksen, George E., Helmuth Wedoe and Gordon Eaton. *Mineral Resources of the Black Range Primitive Area, Grant, Sierra, and Catron Counties, New Mexico.* Geological Survey Bulletin 1319-E, U.S. Government Printing Office, 1970.

U.S.G.S. *Mineral and Water Resources of New Mexico.* Document No. 41-7370, U.S. Government Printing Office, 1965.

Russell, P.L., and W.A. Calhoun. *Niggerhead Manganese Deposit.* Socorro, N M :
U.S. Bureau of Mines Rept. Inv. 4084, 1947

Schilling, J.H. *Molybdenum Resources of New Mexico.* New Mexico Bureau of Mines Bulletin.

Soulé, J.H. *Exploration of Gallinas Fluorspar Deposits.* Lincoln County, NM: U.S. Bureau of Mines Rept. Inv. 3854, 1946.

_____. *Capitan Iron Deposits. Lincoln County, NM: U.S. Bureau of Mines Retp. Inv. 4022, 1947.*

_____. *Silver Spot Manganese-Iron-Zinc Deposits.* Grant County, NM: U.S. Bureau of Mines Rept. Inv. 4217, 1948.

_____. *Investigation of Capitan Iron Deposits.* Lincoln County, NM: U.S. Bureau of Mines Rept. Inv. 4514, 1949.

_____. *Investigation of the Torpedo Copper Deposit, Organ Mining District, Dona Ana County, NM: U.S. Bureau of Mines Rept. Inv. 4791, 1951.*

_____. *Diamond Drilling at Torpedo Copper Mine, Organ Mining District, Dona Ana County, NM: U.S. Bureau of Mines Rept. Inv. 4860, 1952.*

INDEX

www.ingramcontent.com/pod-product-compliance
Lightning Source LLC
Chambersburg PA
CBHW021624270326
41931CB00008B/853